W9-BBY-705

THIS IS NOT A WORK OF FICTION*

*Although *some* poetic license has been taken

PROLOGUE

Out of bed. Remove plugs . . . from ears, wipe crust . . . from eyes.
Log on. Download. Ringer ON. Upload.
Pet cat, Cat. Cat purrs.
Check e-mail.
Flash! AOLInstantMessage©.

Messager is Spinner98, a West Wing White House Staffer who wants to know if I have any 411 on a Congressman the White House believes may have been busted.

Mdrudge: not a word.
Spinner98: nothing about cong. filner being arrested overseas?

I'm not awake two APNewsAlert© minutes and already I'm working both sides of The Hill with a White House request.
"They keep telling me that nobody there bothers to read me," I tell Cat, my one true friend and sometime editor.
"Too gossipy, too unreliable, too mean-spirited," Cat swipes. *"And now they're calling you for confirmation?"*

Spinner98: heard a rumor about it . . . trying to check it out on this end

Mdrudge: i just did a powercheck. i get over fifteen wire services in the drudge newsroom here . . . it didn't happen
Spinner98: you finally getting to earn a living out of this thing?
Mdrudge: lol . . . last mention of filner on any wire on any planet involves a tobacco story . . . 39 minutes ago that did not involve an arrest . . . are you with gore?
Spinner98: i'm a clinton guy . . . been with him since '91.
Mdrudge: did you see insight mag? What a blockbuster
Spinner98: which article you referring to?
Mdrudge: no major starr indictments
Spinner98: i read that in the frontrunner yesterday. didn't make much of a wave around here . . . while the starr probe isn't taken lightly, i think people have written it off for a while now. anything that does come out of it is going to have such a strong political stain that it's tough to see what would come out of it.
Spinner98: when do you start your pool on the bowles replacement? i think you should get some kind of contest going
Mdrudge: isn't it berger
Spinner98: doubt it. strongly doubt it. he has a great reputation around here, but he's not the man.
Mdrudge: did vicky radd tell you she met me at david brock's party?
Spinner98: she told me that she was going . . . of course, she probably didn't admit to you she didn't know what drudge was until about a week before. she's quite a character. I'm not into bad mouthing folks but . . . she definitely wore out her stay with the big guys.
Mdrudge: she was bragging that she could get me a press pass
Spinner98: hmmm . . . not sure why you would want one. you earn your rep. and power from being on the outside
Mdrudge: i just thought when hell broke loose—it would be hot to have one . . . i thought dowd hurt you guys this morning
Mdrudge: have you been in the hot tub?
Spinner98: very funny. i think most every staffer learned about the hot tub in the papers. the dowd story was definitely a slap . . . but it's tough to get upset about her work because she's just so damn creative.

Mdrudge: i had a fun chat with dowd this week at the abc press tour. i did a piece on her for george mag/september

Spinner98: what else you got in the pipeline?

Mdrudge: anything on kathleen willey?

Spinner98: not familiar with her

Mdrudge: she's the one that's been talking with newsweek about . . .

Spinner98: about . . .

Mdrudge: i've got the whole story

Spinner98: not all of us here handle the scandal beat

Mdrudge: isikoff thinks i broke into newsweek's office in dc and stole it off his computer

Spinner98: what's the story?

Mdrudge: pause

Mdrudge: could be explosive

Mdrudge: i think i should just leave you with that name, willey.

Mdrudge: carville, begalla, et al.—would freak if they knew that her name is out there. i tried warnin' the ragin' cajun in the green room at politically incorrect last week, but he kept saying "hoss, whaddya think of the welfare bill?"

Spinner98: lol. yeah, we're all thinking about the welfare bill around here

Mdrudge: david beaubaire—laura capps—julie mason—jason goldberg—jennifer dudley—ana maria dugue—s. naplan—cheryl mills—you know any of these?

Spinner98: i know all of them . . . they all work here . . .

Mdrudge: just a few that I've been told are on my e-mail list

Spinner98: most of them junior staff . . . except for cheryl

Mdrudge: are you junior?

Spinner98: i would say that i'm considered the most senior junior staffer

Spinner98: what's this whilley thing?

Mdrudge: she used to work in the white house—she's talking about publicly accusing clinton of copping a feel in the oval office. sex harassment.

Spinner98: hmmm . . . interesting. are you sure the last name is whilley?

Mdrudge: i am holding off my story on her, because of an urgent request

Spinner98: willey just doesn't seem right to me. i've been here five years and i've never heard the name . . .

"Drudge," Cat interrupts. *"Check it out. All of a sudden he's spelling her name right?!"*
"Duly noted." I smile and continue typing.

Mdrudge: willey—midlothian, va
Mdrudge: she claims that she was a part timer who went to potus bc asking for more work—
Spinner98: i'll check it out. . . .
Spinner98: ok, i'll give you this bit of information. just asked podesta about it and he knows what it is and asked me to check if isikoff was writing for tomorrow on it. he's not, but you knew that.
Spinner98: you and i did not have this conversation. i just got a lot of people very riled up around here about this willey thing. we'll talk later. do not mention this conversation. if asked, i told people that you had on your page: "possible isikoff story on willey" but that it's gone from your page now.
Mdrudge: clear

[SAVE TO FILE]

In a flash, the White House knows that successful as they have been at killing the Isikoff/Willey story, they now have to deal with an internet terrorist whose stock is trade is breaking all the news unfit to print.

Let the future begin!

DRUDGE
MANIFESTO

MATT DRUDGE
with Julia Phillips

NEW AMERICAN LIBRARY

NAL

Published by New American Library, a division of
Penguin Putnam Inc., 375 Hudson Street,
New York, New York 10014, U.S.A.
Penguin Books Ltd, 27 Wrights Lane,
London W8 5TZ, England
Penguin Books Australia Ltd, Ringwood,
Victoria, Australia
Penguin Books Canada Ltd, 10 Alcorn Avenue,
Toronto, Ontario, Canada M4V 3B2
Penguin Books (N.Z.) Ltd, 182–190 Wairau Road,
Auckland 10, New Zealand

Penguin Books Ltd, Registered Offices:
Harmondsworth, Middlesex, England

Published by New American Library, a division of Penguin Putnam Inc.

First New American Library Printing, October 2000
10 9 8 7 6 5

Copyright © Matt Drudge, 2000

All rights reserved

 REGISTERED TRADEMARK—MARCA REGISTRADA

Printed in the United States of America
Set in Helvetica
Designed by Leonard Telesca

Printed in the United States of America

Without limiting the rights under copyright reserved above, no part of this publication may
be reproduced, stored in or introduced into a retrieval system, or transmitted, in any form, or
by any means (electronic, mechanical, photocopying, recording, or otherwise), without the
prior written permission of both the copyright owner and the above publisher of this book.

BOOKS ARE AVAILABLE AT QUANTITY DISCOUNTS WHEN USED TO PROMOTE PRODUCTS OR SERVICES.
FOR INFORMATION PLEASE WRITE TO PREMIUM MARKETING DIVISION, PENGUIN PUTNAM INC.,
375 HUDSON STREET, NEW YORK, NEW YORK 10014.

Dedicated
to
Linda R. Tripp

I'm splurging on a 39-cent taco on Vine Street when I learn I'm being sued by White House aide Sidney Blumenthal for $30,000,000.00.

Mel Karmazin's KFWB 980 newsradio's on my Walkman. LegacyMedia is fading, but I still monitor. Traffic and weather together on the ones. Get rich Get erect Get off commercials are interrupted with a flash: "Cybergossipmonger Matt Drudge today was sued in a DC Federal Court . . ."

Uh-oh.

Am I in hot salsa.

I'd just reported a Washington rumor about Blumenthal, one that Vanity Fair would later acknowledge had been "going around for ten years."

Vanity Fair would not suffer a suit; mine is still pending.

The item was classic Drudge: coverage of the coverage offering dual accounts; a denial next to a charge.

Another radioactive exposure of Washington hypocrisy.

Cat was indisposed when I pushed the ENTER button.

Mistakes were made.*[#A]

Consequently I was forced to retract within twelve hours.

Cat, a black stray I adopted during my CBS Studios tenure, has never let me forget about it.

I finish my meal, refill my mucho grande cerveza de la raiz, and hop into my red Metro Geo, whose balding tires squeal all the way home.

Past Melrose. Santa Monica. Sunset.

I twitch at the Bank of America on the southwest corner where I deposit my nickels and dimes.

In the ten years I've lived here, I've related to these streets so many different ways. I've walked 'em. I've skate-boarded 'em. Bussed 'em. Limousined 'em. I've been chased, but most of the time I'm chasing around and down the boulevards I call home.

Michel LeGrand's Windmills of Your Mind is vibrating from my sound system as I pass Capitol Records. The '68 gem is always in heavy rotation on my homemade travel tapes.

The LeGrand Greats. I've studied every one, and lived a few.

What Are You Doing the Rest of Your Life? How Do You Keep the Music Playing? Between Yesterday and Tomorrow.

This is One of Those Moments.

Zoom up the hill at Yucca, a dormant volcano, the Hollywood Reporter headlined the week of the Northridge Quake.

Hit the sharp left at Franklin. Pop out the LeGrand.

Punch in the Bambaataa, Planet Rock. Geo Power.

For a second I choke.

Can a judge take away my wheels when I can't come up with the $30 mil?

I race to my apartment—my newsroom—fire up the machines.

First headline I see, Reuters A-Wire Flash already in its 2nd write-thru: "Clinton Gore Approved of Filing Libel Suit." Hmm.

Payback.

Two weeks ago, I broke a story on the daisy named Willey (who'd accused POTUS of picking her petals in a hallway off the Oval), which Michael Isikoff eventually got into print eight days later.

I check with my receptionist, an AT&T 1872 2-line digital answering system. Forty-nine messages.

Play. Stop. Forward. Repeat.

All the networks. All the newspapers. All the wires.

Bouncing beams from dish to dish, e-mails, faxes, and alarms. Cellphones. Conference calls. Coming Soons. Press releases rumor innnuendo hot tips blind items hype—everything we are, everything we've ever been—a mixed multimedia martini, served up on the EveningNews Happy Hour. The anticipointment of it all.

All. Delete.

I hit the mailbox at drudgereport.com.

6735 messages left to download. Cancel.

For the first time in American history a sitting president has approved a civil action against a reporter. And it's me.

This is the sort of trick one might have expected from Nixon. Dick. Though Nixon was more talk than action and Clinton is not.

At least when it comes to silencing his critics.

"You're the only one they are afraid of, they can't control you," Mary Carville Matalin Instant Messages on AOL. "Are you alright, Drudge? You can come out to Virginia. I'll hide you here on the farm."

Sweet Shenandoah Mary.

"Thanks, I'd better not. Your husband will call a hog slaughter after he turns me in to the pigs at Williams & Connolly!"

"Mr. Blumenthal *did* talk to the president and the vice-president about this, who told him that they support him—" Joe Lockhart slips while addressing reporters at a Martha's Vineyard elementary school.

Joe's imbibed too much mucho grande cerveza de la raiz, I think.

Whatever.

Sued by the White House, my latest online adventure.

"You're not being sued by the White House, that's absurd," Michael Kinsley, who once tried to recruit me for Microsoft, mocks during a joint appearance on C-SPAN.

But Lockhart *is* actively involved in the litigation.

Susan Estrich writes a pro-Drudge Op-Ed for USA Today and Lockhart calls the paper to complain. I'm flattered, but one would think the prez's press secretary has more important things to do with his time.

Susan is so infuriated she writes a second piece:

> I raised questions in a column about whether the main-stream media—which was savagely drubbing Matt Drudge for having made a mistake which he retracted, as if none of them ever had—might in fact be currying favor with the White House's communications man by doing so. Blumenthal had the White House press office complain to USA Today about me.

Other West Wingers quickly get into the act.

White House Aide Sean Johnson, for example, calls reporter Tucker Carlson, the boy with the ice cream face, asking for his home address. Carlson assumes he is being invited to a White House fête, but instead he is served with a subpoena from Blumenthal.

Former NewYorkerNewRepublicWashingtonPost journalist Sidney Blumenthal is hunting down suspected sources.

"You can't use the White House Press Office for a private lawsuit," Carlson cries.

Oh yes you can.

Sidney Blumenthal wants to exact from me the exact amount exacted from OJSimpson by an exacting civil jury for double murder.

Exactly.

Well, he's welcome to try.

Warren Beatty, who's probably worth far more, tells me at a party at Spago that he wonders if, in the near future, there'll be any basis for libel and defamation.

"The I-N-T-E-R-N-E-T," he intones sagely, as if I don't know. "Anyone from anywhere can cover anything . . ."

"And be sued by everyone!"

"What type of computer do you use?" Jeffrey Katzenburg asks, patting my back as he shakes my hand.

"Who's gonna play you in the movie?" Dustin Hoffman says as we pick from the trays.

"Carl Bernstein," I say before I think.

"You're one of the most important guys in the country, and you need to be more stimulated," Entertainment Attorney Bert Fields pronounces.

"No, you're one of the most important guys in the country 'cause you're going to get Mr. Katzenberg his $300 million."

They laugh at my boldness.

"I think the story you did on Al Gore burning all of that jet fuel to get to the Global Warming summit was just great." Hoffman smiles.

"You're Matt Drudge?" Larry King challenges and frowns.

"Meeting you is my biggest thrill since meeting John Wayne," Warren says. I take him at his word.

"Thank you."

"How's Sidney Blumenthal?" Annette jabs, envious of the attention, fixing me with the same cold stare she gave

John Cusack, working on her back in a raw sex scene. (The Grifters.)

I can relate.

I get turned on, too, every time I pass the Taco Bell down on Vine and I remember those 39-cent tacos. Indigestion on the ones.

"The enemies of the Future are always the very nicest people."
—Christopher Morley—05/03/39
Kitty Foyle, Chapter 5

"Any time an individual . . . leaps so far . . . ahead . . . and throws a system . . . out of balance . . . you've got a problem."
—Hillary—3:16 pm—02/11/98
Map Room, The White House

"This is really boring."
—Katie Couric—12:20 am—01/01/00
Times Square, NBC

[BOOT UP]

This is the most exciting moment in the history of News.
Any*one* from any*where* can cover any*thing*.
And send it out to *everyone*.

Reports on last hour's 8.7-mag. quake in The Kodiak Islands
of Alaska, tomorrow's firing of ConnieChung from THECBS-
EVENINGNEWS, or next week's NEWSWEEK's spiking of a
piece on past presidential predilection for penile pumping by
plump, politically placed, postpubescent White House Pretties
can be dispatched faster than an intercontinental blistered nuke.
Fired from Pakistan, compliments of U.S. tech stolen by
China, sold to Iran, transferred from Russia on Taiwanese hardware processed by Israeli software.

Hey, it's The Zeroes.
Just hit the ENTER button.
I have. And lived to sell the tale.

If I'm not interesting, the world's not interesting.
If the DRUDGE REPORT is boring, the world is boring.

It's Zero, Babies.

And if I'm boring, you're boring.

24 hours a day, 7 days a week, 365 days a 12-month year, 10 years a decade, 10 decades a century, and 10 centuries a millennium, as far as a chip can see, wire services from all over the world move raw data . . . all over the world!

I can access, edit, headline and . . . link to it all!

Throw it up on a website and wait for you to come.

For seven premillennial years, I've covered the world from my Hollywood apartment, dressed in my drawers.

I've reported when, how, and what I've wanted.

My only limitations have been those I've created.

There's been no editor, no lawyer, no judge, no president to tell me I can't.

And there never will be.

Technology has finally caught up with individual liberty.

On the boulevards, we call it "freedom of the brain."*[#1]

In this post–satellite dish era—when individuals can broadcast their wetdreams with neither a license nor a handbook of regulations issued by Government—The Elites, fearing loss of power, see chaos and anarchy.

I see only sunshine. The world is interesting. I'm interesting.

You're interesting.*[#2]

It all starts with the wires. It all ends with the wires.

Information being power and all.

A random Associated Press NewsAlert© begets CNN-BreakingNews© begets Reuters© begets Rush Limbaugh©. If the Alert™ becomes A Story after 157 minutes, it'll beget 20/20DatelineEntertainmentTonight60Minutes®. If it lasts 3¹/₄ days, it'll run above the fold in TheNewYorkTimes® and below in TheNationalEnquirer™. Give it two weeks and someone at the New Yorker© will pound out a rewrite, win a Pulitzer©. A month, and ScottRudinSherryLansingHarveyWeinstein(sm) options it for PaltrowDamonWoo® *or* P.T. Anderson©, thinking Oscar© just as David E. Kelley©, demanding Emmy, races a secret script for a series starring SomeoneSuperSkinny(PatentPending). Still bouncing in six months? Billboard© pronounces SonyMottola-LaurynHill's© rap will wrap up Grammy®. A year in, PrNews-wire© reports DonDeLillo's© handed in his first 1000 pages on a guaranteed National Book Award Winner® that began . . . with the stray AP NewsAlert© a thousand cycles ago.

Welcome to the Zeroes, pal.

You'll get it where you want it.

The buffet's bigger than at WynnBellagio©.

I like to start my meal with the XINHUA wire from China mixed with KYODO from Japan.

A soupçon of AGENCE FRANCE-PRESSE stirred with ITAR-TASS from Moscow.

ISLAMIC REPUBLIC wire for curry and the JERUSALEM POST for matzoh.

NORTH KOREAN CENTRAL NEWS AGENCY when it's cold.

UK's PRESSASSOCIATION when it's wet.

AdAgeDeadlineE!ChannelBskyBBBCFoxNews if I'm lonely.

DeutschePresse-AgenturMSNBCHollywoodReporter when I'm blue.

It's always waiting for you.*[#3]

Anywhere you want it. You can get it.

For the first time in the history of communication, you don't have to live in a corporate "newsroom" for access to instant information. With a modem, a phone jack, and an inexpensive computer, your newsroom can be your living room, your bedroom . . . your bathroom, if you're so inclined.*[#4]

You can take on the Big Boys between flushes.*[#5]

You can beat CNN to the announcement of Princess Diana's death by eight minutes, as I once did, thanks to an e-tip from a reporter on the scene.*[#6] As They debate, edit, rewrite, fix 'n' figure what the *real* slant is, you've reported it and graduated it.

Dished it, dismissed it, and moved it.

Sitting in the WashingtonPost Newsroom, which is the size of a football field, watching layers of lawyers, editors, and corporate newsies at work, I asked top media reporter Howard Kurtz, a Postie who cooks it in a cubbie: "They need all this to please The Bubbie?"

In the background, thousands of people type on thousands of keyboards to meet one deadline to produce one newspaper servicing one town. DC. My home. Capital City.

What a place to grow up in.

I walked the streets. Aimless teen. Young adult.

Studying The Power I believed emanated from every building. Negotiated in every restaurant. Congregated on every corner.

Every time, it seemed, I'd end up at the WashingtonPost Newsroom on 15th. I'd look up longingly, knowing I'd never get in. Didn't attend the right schools. Never enjoyed any school, in fact. My father was not the son of a famous drunken Southern senator, nor was I even remotely connected to a powerful publishing dynasty.

My sneaks weren't *Grahams*.

Burning I may have been, but I was sophisticated enough to know I would never be granted any access, obtain any credentials, get that meeting with Vernon Jordan.

I come from a typical American family.

Bob and Claire Drudge divorced when I was six.

Dad, a social worker, shacked up with Someone New and moved to the east coast of Maryland. I stayed with Mom, one of the first women to graduate from Catholic University Law School and pass the Bar in Maryland. She took a full-time job.

No brothers. No sisters.

Even though I spent a lot of time alone, I enjoyed the support and friendship of a loosely knit neighborhood gang with whom I've consciously lost touch. What can I say?

I make friends easily. Keeping them is . . . difficult.

Talk radio tucked me in at night and the police scanner was my unconditional best friend. We remain pals to this day.

Who says I can't maintain a longterm personal relationship?

Of course, Mom overcompensated.

Clarinet lessons. Ridiculous.

Hebrew school. Hey Nun Vuv is the most I absorbed in four painfully long years.

I failed Bar Mitzvah.

I wasn't much better in secular (i.e., sexular) school, which was like jail to me. D in Current Events. E in just about everything else.

Barely graduated Class of '84.

341st out of 355, more than adequate curriculum vitae for a post at 7-Eleven.

Then, there were the babysitting chores, which I've expunged from memory. My charges, however, have not—as evidenced by a March '98 page-one headline in the venerable Takoma Voice, whose motto is "The truth is rarely pure and never simple." (Oscar Wilde.)

Exclusive! I Was Babysat by Matt Drudge!

"I was seven or eight and he was about five years older than me," began Cari Weisman. "He used to get me and some other kids on this tire-swing and really scare us. He made it go too high. But even when he did, I trusted him. We went trick-or-treating and he took us all over the neighborhood, much farther than I would have been allowed to go. He'd take all the kids to a creek behind my house when it was dark and tell us all these elaborate stories. We'd be terrified. A lot of parents thought he was obnoxious [but] he was wonderful."

There wasn't much likelihood of upward mobility in my swing shift position at 7-Eleven.

Although the gig did have more fringe benefits than just testing the Slurpee machine and dating a hot batch of nachos.

Every morning at about 2 o'clock the bulldog editions of all the major papers would be dropped off right at my doorstep.

I couldn't wait to get my hands on them.

While the rest of the city slept, I'd read fresh headlines and bylines—first, before anyone else.

The predawn customers would get an earful.

I was never sure why I cared about being first, but boy did I feel connected when I was. And the job was sure easier than my previous paychecks: packing groceries and selling Time-Life books over the telephone. Or my other rewarding experience in media: delivering the late great Washington Star in my Takoma Park, Maryland, neighborhood.

Each day after junior high school, I would load up the cart and hit the sidewalks. Newspaperboy Drudge. The circulation department at the Star gave me way too many streets to service. Most days I wouldn't get to each and every address on my route.

That might've been because I stopped to read the entire paper on a park bench one block from my house before I even started.

On the bench, I would play editor.

I noticed how *their* lead story was not really *the* lead story. How the hottest news was buried on the inside pages and the best reporting was riding at the end of the copy when it should have been at the beginning.

I'd rewrite my own headlines for an audience of one.

Not counting the squirrels.

On the day President Reagan was shot, the *Star* header was far too wordy. I just knew I'd do it better if I were in charge.

Sooo . . . in the famous words of another newsman, Horace Greeley: I, still a young man, went West.

Out to Hollywood—and I do mean Hollywood, not Beverly Hills, not the Palisades, no 90210 or 90265 for this kid—the part of Hollywood they're always promising to clean up and never do.

The Hollywood featured nightly in *Cops* and *When Animals Attack*. Murdoch's Hollywood. As appropriated by Less Moonves.

Survivor: I swung into another clerk job. This time, at CBS Studios.

7-Eleven burritos became Beverly Blvd. Babes and Price Is Right showcases.

Living large under Lou Dorfman's logo, the infamous EYE, I folded T-shirts in their gift shop, dusted off 60 Minutes coffee mugs, dined daily in the commissary, indulged in after-hours conversations with the ghost of Bill Paley.

It was during one of these chats that he reminded me the first step in good reporting—is good snooping.

Inspired, I went out of my way to service executive suites, listening carefully to whispered conversation, intercepting the occasional memo. Stalking the newsroom.

I hit paydirt when I discovered the trash cans in the Xerox room at Television City, located on the ground floor—NE corner. They were stuffed to the brim each morning with Nielsen ratings—late-century gold if I got in before the cleaning crew fed the shredders. I tracked their schedule and beat them by twenty minutes every day.

I thought I was on the move—but my father worried I was in a giant stall. In a parental panic, he overcame his fear of flying and dropped by for a visit. At the end of his stay, during the drive to the airport, sensing some action was called for, he dragged me to a stripmall off Sunset.

"C'mon," he said desperately. "I'm getting you a computer."

"Oh, yeah, and what am I gonna do with that?"

As they say at TVCity, CUT TO: Months later . . .

I found a way to post items on Internet newsgroups, things I had gleaned direct from the soundstages, the halls and the stalls.

I collected a few e-mail addresses.

I set up a list.

One reader turned into five.

Five into a hundred.

And faster than you can say I NEVER HAD SEXUAL RE-LATIONS WITH THAT WOMAN, it was a thousand, five thousand, a hundred thousand.

The ensuing website practically launched itself.

I called it the DRUDGE REPORT. Built by Radio Shack.

In 1999, it had 240,778,230 visits. In 2000, it's projected to have over 350,000,000.

But a million isn't what it used to be.

No need for the football field, Kurtz, to be one of the biggest news operations in America. Even less need for those layers of lawyers working Lobster Alley.

Access, edit, headline and . . . link to it all!

Who knows? One day you might end up on The Washington Post's roof, like me, having your Tootsie moment, being photographed for yet another Style Section spread, Sunday, above the fold.*[#7]

Snap! Snap! Snap! Pop! Pop! Pop!

"The man with the Dickensian name has changed American culture more than the culture has changed him," the Post tattooed on dead trees.

Closer. Closer to the camera, please.

Snap! Snap! Snap!

"The DRUDGE REPORT has become the buzz of the media-industrial complex."

Pop! Pop! Pop! Tilt the hat.

Snap! Snap! Snap! Yeah, like that.

"Suddenly, without warning, he is white hot."

Loosen the tie. Pop!

Now look up at the sky. Snap!

"Executive Editor Leonard Downie, Jr. cordially invites you . . ."

Left. Pop! Right. Snap!

Closer. Closer. Closer.

Smile. Frown. Up. Down.

Laugh. Flash!

Always.

Laugh.

Modem, phone jack . . . inexpensive computer.

Any*thing* from any*where* out to *everyone*.

Okay. I confess. I *do* run copy by Cat all the time.

Constantly by my side, Cat's been around for almost every DRUDGE REPORT.

Always there for me, smiling, telling me how great I am.

"Don't get carried away, Drudge. They throw you from that roof once they pick their favorite shots. Your pal Limbaugh at EIB near PBI says, 'First you're a curiosity (and as you always say, Maha-Rushie says you are to the internet what he is to broadcasting) . . . Then you're sought out. Then you're praised. They write about you. They build you up. Then, they tear you down. Down. Down. Down. Splat!' And didn't 'Mr. Cordially Invites' give you a shiner on C-SPAN? Didn't he say, 'Matt Drudge is no longer thought of as a journalist, by anyone. He's seen as an entertainer, of sorts.' "

"Oh, Cat, Downie's an entertainer of sorts, too. Just hours after that C-SPAN he had to issue a flash apology: 'A Washington Post article about New Jersey mistakenly said former governor Brendan Byrne is deceased.' "

"Sssssssssssss!"

"Shut up, Cat, or I'm gonna post pornographic Polaroids of you on the web and upload your meows to Napster."

"You shut up or I'm e-ing your Polaroids and .MP3s to Johnson at Page Six. Cc-ed to Coz, Walls, Frost, Fink, Smith, Grove, even David Talbot, if he's still in business . . . am I missing anyone . . . ?"

"Have you been peeping in my black book again, Cat . . . ?"

"Yes, 'cause if someday someone gets a judgment, I may have to tell the stories I've killed just to buy your FancyFeast . . ."

"Well, you're the one who's addicted to Sheba . . ."

". . . and may I state, for the record, I'm constantly by your side so you don't go too far over the line, not to mention, forget to feed me . . ."

World: never boring. Drudge: always interesting.

Cat: always there.

The DRUDGE REPORT has been headline, tagline, and punch-line since its debut: winter 1994.

Out of the gate, I was breaking and making news.

From a little corner in my Hollywood hovel, in the company of nothing more than my 486 Packard Bell computer, I become a player, consistently able to break big stories.

Thanks to a growing network of sources.

The Drudge Report, first to name the vice-presidential nominee in '96. A source close to Dole called from a houseboat anchored off San Diego.

First to report Jerry Seinfeld would ask for a million dollars a week or he would walk. A show source came into the gift shop at Studio Center with a tape of Seinfeld ranting in his office.

A new cable network is forming? I was first to report the unholy alliance between Microsoft and NBC. A Saturday Night Live director overheard network honcho Bob Wright in the elevator and scurried back up to his office to e-mail.

Buchanan is surging and would likely win New Hampshire. John Sununu picked for the Crossfire chair. Dan Rather will be told in the morning that his co-anchor is being dropped. My So-Called Life will not be returning in the Fall. Clinton will take his Paula Jones fight to the Supreme Court. The West Coast & Alaska Tsunami Warning Center has issued a tidal wave alert after a 7.2-mag. quake rocked Kuril Islands twenty minutes prior.

First. First. First.

Mixing up the genres. Politics? Important as Hollywood.

Which is as important as Science.

Visitor logs for the Drudge Report website showed visits from all over: senate.gov, nasa.gov, nytimes.com, disney.com, suck.com., house.gov, onion.com, doj.gov.

First every weekend with boxoffice results that even studio executives admitted they got from me. I broke the B.O. reports so early that an executive from Warner Bros. threatened me with legal action, complaining that I was creating negative publicity, publishing bad numbers and misreporting WB's B.O. performance. (They spend all week with the support press—Entertainment Tonight, E! Channel, Entertainment LastWeekly, US, People, New York Times—hyping the latest "smash hit." Then I come along early Saturday morning to post the overnights on the internet and expose that the audience failed to show.) I told the executive I'd be happy to remove Warner movies from my Friday night list. "You can't remove our movies from your list, that'll hurt us more," said the Suit. What Bugs Bunny didn't know . . . I just called the William Morris Agency's gross hotline (compliments of a Drudge reader) and posted their numbers! A huge draw. Questioned under oath, White House communications aide/litigant Blumenthal would swear he began reading the website for boxoffice.

"Like Walter Winchell before him, Drudge catches the public's attention with wit, humor and gimmicky presentations about the Washington–New York–Los Angeles power grid," wrote Rita Ciolli in Newsday, October 1996. "Drudge maximizes the internet's potential to make the news cycle timeless and boundless."

"The news comes at me, but I can't predict when," I explained to Media & the Law a few weeks later. "That's why I give myself the ability to file when I want rather than every day or at a certain time. Technology lets me be independent. I've got no budget, no bosses, no deadline."

This is before the Washington Post has a website, or the New York Daily News, or the New York Times, or CNN, or Daily Variety—which, by the way, rides early in the evening on Reuters circuits for next-day cycles.

I'm a new creature, lifting off the wires—e.g., embargoed Los Angeles Times feeds—and making big headlines from their yet-to-be published goodies.

I employ killer apps for online news.

My website turns into the best place to catch breaking newsbreaks and headlines before they're published.

Within a year of my launch, I inspire cover stories and of course, I cover them, too, usually before they fill the racks with dead trees.

I'm even a few jumps ahead of the hardworking clerks at 7-Eleven.

I've been rhymed and slimed and told to get out of town while I still had my life for daring to confront the mainstream types so accustomed to total control.*[#8]

I took hits from the Left:

"There is such a level of built-in irresponsibility in everything he does," cried First Amendment Protector Floyd Abrams on a Wall Street Journal Page One.

"Drudge is the troll under the bridge of Internet journalism," Slate slammed.

"Drudge had sex with eggs," sneaked MSNBC's Jeanette Walls.

I took hits from the Right:

"Drudge has been smoking funny cigarettes," Arizona Senator John McCain fumed when I first reported that he would be rolling out papers to file for his presidential candidacy.

"I'd give him a journalistic beating, a legal beating, and a physical beating," huffed Steve Dunleavy of CurrentAffairNewYorkPost.

The more hits I took, the more hits I got.

XXX DRUDGE REPORT XXX
OCTOBER 20, 1995 13:30 UTC XXX

MURDOCH MAG SMASHES NET

WASHINGTON—The Murdoch-monied magazine WEEKLY STANDARD has just declared war on the internet with next week's cover story angrily titled, "Smash The Internet." Executive editor David Brooks calls the story an "anti-cyberspace article on the dangerous flow of inaccurate information you find all over the net."

Cover art: a sledgehammer smashing a computer monitor.

Translation: our new magazine is having trouble with sales and we feel the internet is getting in the way of our ability to garner an audience. Attack mode.

What are Murdoch, Fred Barnes and Bill Kristol up to? Why attack the internet? Why does the power structure—in this case, the Republican mafia—find it disturbing that citizens are gathering information via new media? And why do the "know-it-alls" find it hard to trust the reader to find truth from internet sources?

XXX

Four years later, aging Media Tycoon Murdoch, who's either constantly exposed to Saint Bart's sun, Bain de Soleil instant-tanning lotion, or who travels in full TV makeup, would seal his conversion to the internet in a speech at Oxford, painting a picture of a bright tech future hampered only by meddling governments and industry. "I am not among those who fear the new technology," Murdoch proclaimed. He predicted a strong future for new and existing BrandNames. "In my own business, change is so rapid that you take a holiday at your peril. You might return to find a changed world," he said. "Change is not only accelerating, its direction and consequences are becoming less predictable. Central planning is a dangerous game."

Stop the presses!

Rupert Discovers Sliced Bread!

*   *   *

The more hits I got, the more hits I got.*[#9]

I've accrued a pile of Lexis Nexis clips (keyword: Drudge) reaching higher than any skyscraper on Sixth Avenue. Since Nexis is blood racing through the vena cava of LegacyMedia I'm sought out—even venerated—by the very people who trash me.

I have little ambition, but they make me famous.

Which is interesting.

And infamous. Not boring.

Notorious. Even better.

Television is so over, but I've been on:

MeetThePressLettermanWashingtonJournalExtra!P.I.Crossfire-NightlineLeezaTodayEntertainmentTonight(3CoverStories)Reliable-Sources.

Print's way finished, but I've been in:

TheNewYorkTimesNationalEnquirerLosAngelesTimesGlobe-WashingtonPostStarVanityFairNationalExaminerTimeMadNews-week . . .

Manners are history, so I'll get back to:

60MinutesBostonGlobeUSATodayVarietyDailyVarietyVariety .comSalonChicagoTribDallasMorningNewsContentPunchTalk-Feed . . .

Who cares, but I've never heard from:

NewYorkReviewofBooksScientificAmericanNewEnglandJournal-ofMedicineArchitecturalDigestWeeklyWorldNewsWomen'sWear-Daily . . .

The above-referenced entities consider themselves royalty, but they're rapidly being replaced by 21-year-old Barons with Browsers and 14-year-old Dukes with Databases and 7-year-old Princesses with Printouts.

They are old, old, old.

But no one's told them yet.

Dead. Dead. Dead.

They haven't read their obits on the internet.

"Click your heels three times and I'll get you there," Mark Halperin of ABC News says confidently over the phone in my up-graded suite at the toney Mayflower Hotel. "What's your social security number? We'll run it through. Be at the gate at 1:30."

Oooh . . . this is exciting!

I ASKJEEVES.com how to mix a cosmopolitan, stirred not shaken, and break open the wet bar. I'm not a drinker, but I may as well spend the $12.95 before Sidney and Joe get their hands on it.

Social security number for entrée to the White House? For the daily press briefing? Didn't the Feds promise that social security numbers would never be used for ID?

Maybe I should ask Mike McCurry about that.

Halperin and his ABC pal, Josh Gerstein, cornered me at a dinner a couple of weeks ago, offering an invite to the White House.

"Maybe a presidential press conference. Do you have a wire-less remote? Could you file during the press conference? Beat Wolf Blitzer?" the intrigued Halperin stroked.

"I've filed from nearly everywhere else."

"How?"

"Anywhere there's a phone connection. You have no idea how many Drudge Reports I've generated from airport payphones fill-ing the time between delays. Last week, I teased the big Gerth story in the Times three hours before they published it—live from Houston."

"Wow."

It dawns on me I have a large DC cult following, especially the electronic media types. Halperin, a close-personal-friend of George Stephanopolous (sans the Acropolis) thinks he'll make history with me on location at 1600 Penn. What can I say? This is a guy whose office is lined with tabloid headlines starring Dick Morris.

I grab a quick anxiety-shower, don my summer costume: white shirt by Sears, black tie by Gap, tan suit by Brooks, Walkman by Sony, homemade Radiohead travel-tape by Drudge. And my beloved black Florsheims, which have transported me up Hollywood boulevards, down Sin City's Fremont, across Empire's 34th, over to State-Street-that-great-street, and back to my hometown, the Capital, which is becoming smaller with each visit.

Social Security card at the ready, I strut down Connecticut Avenue. The Bank thermometer reads 97 degrees.

It's been this way for days.

Radiohead's Fitter Happier vibrates through my radio head.

"Getting on better with your associate employee/contemporaries . . ." The late-'90s gem is heavily rotated on my tape. The Radiohead greats. I've studied every one and lived a few. Exit Song. Karma Police. Fake Plastic Trees. Creep.

I pass Farragut Square, wave at the Old Gray Lady on Eye Street, sniff the Bombay Club where DOPOTUS Chelsea often veggie-curry platters. Through Lafayette Park over to 17th.

I spot Wolf Blitzer simultaneously with some passing fans who actually lean out of their car to scream: "It's Wolf Blitzer!" The "senior of the senior" White House correspondents (as he once described himself to USA Today) waves at them happily.

I spot a protestor carrying a sign that reads:

Treason is the Reason.

I spot the West Gate.

Secret Service spot me.

Two blasé agents wave me through with nary a glance.

I'm certainly not as pretty as Eleanor Mondale, but I am the first internet reporter granted access to the hallowed halls of eop.gov.

My heart races when I reach the other side of the fence.

I'm in!

I'm already soaked through but I walk up the driveway at a brisk aerobic pace, pass Rita Braver—to whom I once priority-overnighted a 48 Hours mug and a Bold and Beautiful T-shirt—on my way into the pressroom.

I nearly collide with Helen Thomas, UPI Wire Queen, dressed in urgent red from head to toe.

I look around.

I'm surrounded by the stars of The White House Press Corps, faces I know from years of tracking C-SPAN's Washington Journal.

I'm pretty sure nobody recognizes me.

A bank of cameras line the back of the room, maybe two dozen rows of movie-theater seats fill the rest. It's smaller than I thought.

I stand off to the side in back, crunched against broadcast paraphernalia, which affords me a low profile, a full view of the room, and the players therein.

Helen's in the front row.

Rita's in the fifth.

Blitzer, the most "senior of the senior," is in the sixth next to Gerstein, who acknowledges me with a small wink.

"Looks like we've got a holiday crowd here," Mike McCurry starts. "I like that. Early departure. I'm in favor of it. The problem is, I'm going to run into all of you on I-95 going up to the Jersey shore this afternoon."

The assemblage is plotting its Fourth of July getaway.

Terry Hunt from the AP, probably another I-95er, checks his watch every two seconds. A Reuters dude winds his.

But first, a little attention to the plight of the extremely poor.

Question #1: "What's the big news on welfare reform?"

In the middle of the room, prominently displayed, a middle-aged woman even I can't ID. She holds up her compact mirror, smears on purple lipstick. Then powder. Now blush!

She appears completely oblivious to her surroundings.

Follow-up: "Does the President's plan cover all low-income working families, Mike?"

The woman flosses her teeth.

Tweezes and reaches for a Q-tip.

Our eyes and ears on the Executive Branch.

I check around the room.

Nobody in the overlit scene is as preoccupied as I am with this broad's odd behavior, never mind her mental health.

Isn't this room only for press?

Aren't the people here the chosen few, the ones we rely on for information? Keepers of The Fourth Estate?

How many reporters would kill to get into this room? Have questions for the White House but no access? Who aren't issued credentials? Whose social security numbers ain't clean enough.

Who don't consider this pressroom an air-conditioned pitstop en route to Rehoboth.

Some center of power! Some representation of the people.

Next question: "The agreement that Ukraine is going to sign, will that give them a relationship with NATO equal to that of Russia?"

I try to pay attention to his answer but the mystery woman puts her compact in her purse and extracts manicure/pedicure apparatus. She commences to file the nails on her right hand.

"The structure of that arrangement is very similar to the one that was developed with the Russian Federation . . ." McCurry drones, and I can't help myself, I just have to check out Ms. Rehoboth . . .

Omigod! She's moved to her feet!

Nobody else notices, which only makes me more obsessed.

Question: "Is the President meeting with Secretary General Solana on Monday?"

Ms. R. inserts turqoise Styrofoam separators between the toes of her left foot, and commences Van Gogh–ing that same horrible puce-purple.

I laugh out loud and must exit the brief-room for a brief time-out. I wander into the rundown pressroom down the hall, the one that isn't televised.

Fading carpet. Worn-out keyboards.

I'm alone with the machines.

I search for and locate the UPI cubbyhole.

It all starts with the wires.

I search for and locate Helen Thomas's terminal.

It all ends with the wires.

I take a seat. I take a peek.

Information being power and all.

Surprisingly, Helen's computer looks like an old Commodore-style. Helen's Backstairs at the White House. Helen's Washington Windows.

I type in a header: "Today, Matt Drudge was bestowed an

Honorary Doctorate at the Columbia School of Journalism for his groundbreaking internet reporting."*[#10]

For a moment I consider hitting the Enter button, but I can hear from down the hall that McCurry's winding down.

I backspace to Prompt. What waaaas I thinking?

I trot back in.

Yes!

I've got a question.

"Mike," I begin without identifying myself, "in recent weeks Ken Starr has been shopping a book proposal with major publishing houses in New York."

McCurry: "Oh, do tell."

Laughter.

"It's titled 'Mike McCurry,' " Ms. Fingers&Toes quips, blithely blowing on her nails. Hands, not feet.

Mmmmm, so she is paying attention. Multitasking.

More laughter.

"It's a book proposal," I continue, "not relating to Whitewater . . ."

"Aaaagh," McCurry says.

"The perception in New York is that he's cashing in on his celebrity, and I understand the money may be moving upwards. Would you have any comment at this point?"

"Naaagh," McCurry jabs, fixing me with the same cold stare as Annette Bening did at Spago—not to mention Peter Gallagher, working on her back in a raw sex scene. (American Beauty.)

Braver darts from her chair, nearly ripping her hose, and heads hurriedly for the back. UPI's Helen T rushes me.

Details. Gimme details.

I introduce myself. "Hello, Helen, I'm Matt Drudge. I write a column on the—"

"I know who you are. Tell me more . . ."

"All I know, Helen, is Starr's typed up some sort of proposal for a book about constitutional law."

"Very good," she says, and smiles benignly.

We travel toward her terminal together and I notice for the first time the sorry state of the heavily stained, smelly hallway carpet. Memo to Hillary: Buy Nature's Miracle.

"I'm going to file a story on this book proposal," Helen says. "Catcha later."

"Later?"

"3:30. You know, the Vet-Event in the East Room."

No, I don't know. But I'm prepared to go with the flow.

I sidle over to Mr. AP NewsAlert himself, Terence Hunt.

"Mr. Hunt, I'm Matt Drudge."

"I know . . ."

"I love your work."

"I check your webpage sometimes." He smiles.

I'm face-to-face with the most powerful computer in the info-universe, the AP Machine at eop.gov.

This machine *starts* the cycles. All things White House begin here. The copy I receive in my built-by-Radio-Shack Hollywood newsroom is written here. By this man. In this cubbyhole.

When he hits the ENTER button hundreds of outlets feel it.

Hundreds aren't thousands and thousands aren't millions and millions aren't what they used to be. But still.

It all starts with the wires.

"When you issue a news alert, how long does it take to get going? What's the ETA on the A-Wire?"

"Pretty fast."

"Can you go out live?" I ask. "If, say, something really huge happened?"

"I think I figured out a way. I'd have a few minutes before anybody at the home office would notice. I've thought a lot about what I'm going to write the day I decide to leave," he jokes.

It all ends with the wires.

In the CBS stall Rita Braver whispers urgently into her phone, "I don't know what it's about."

I creep up behind her, convinced she's discussing my flash with her husband Bob Barnett, book agent and lawyer to Clinton, Hillary Rodham, Woodward, Bob, and Couric, CuteKatie.

Among Others.

"Matt Drudge is here. Hold on a second."

She knows who I am? Why does that *not* make me feel good.

"I know who you're talking to, Rita," I say.

"Oh no no no no. No. Oh no. No, it's not . . ." Busted?

Reporters who marry lawyers who work for clients who have sex with presidents, among others . . .

Gerstein pulls me into the ABC stall next door.

"Worried I'm gonna connect the dots?" I ask.

"I just wanted to introduce you to Anne Compton."

"Are you repped by Bob Barnett? Perchance?"

They check their watches, avoiding my eyes.

"Time for the Vet-Event!" Anne says merrily, and we link arms.

"Off to see the wizard," I sing, and they pretend to laugh.

3:29 pm ET
East Room, The White House

The room is jammed and stuffy.

No airconditioning could keep up with this heatwave.

A band plays Grand Old Flag and other patriotic ditties, but I can't get Radiohead's Fitter Happier out of my skull.

Lead singer Thom York has said the song is the most escapist cut on his OK Computer CD. "We put the lyrics in the computer with Talk program—just standard software. The text is now spoken by an emotionless computer voice. I see it as the ultimate disassociation with the lyrics and my responsibility for them."

The multitude quiets as Clinton/Gore makes its entrance.

Hard to say about the Prez, but the Vice Prez is in full make-up, TV ready. I one-eighty this way and that, and indeed the broadcast paraphernalia is in full red-light mode.

The Prez dutifully recites what feels like *his* computer-generated lyrics: "Mr. Vice President, Commander Frank, Colonel Harmon, Secretary Albright, Secretary Cohen, Ambassador Richardson, Mr. Berger, General Shalikashvili, General Ralston, and Members of the Joint Chiefs, to the distinguished veterans and citizens . . . tomorrow we will commemorate Independence Day and The Declaration of Independence . . ." But I hear:

"Fitter happier and more productive.

"A pig in a cage on antibiotics."

I pace the back of the room, skirting the edge of the crowd and find a corner window offering a great view of 16th Street. As a kid, I used to cut school to stand on the other side, looking in.

Now, I'm looking out.

And up.

Oh dear. Cobwebs.

Memo to Hill: Buy Dustbuster.

Another thing. These drapes clash with the art.

And by the way, I don't think I like it here.

Press Conference legend Sarah McClendon, wheelchair-bound, snoozes, snoring. Her shirt has slipped off her shoulder and down her arm, revealing one fleshtone brastrap.

Clinton gives good chin.

Alison Mitchell of The New York Times gives me bad look.

I wonder how many times a day she checks my page.

"We have a lot to celebrate on this July 4th. We are at peace. We are more prosperous than we have been in a generation, our liberty more secure than ever . . ."

To my left, Wolf Blitzer.
I catch his eye and he pretends not to see.
That's okay, you old kibitzer, you're only on TV.
To my right, Shipman, Claire, who frowns at me.
Glare Claire glare, *you* had to propose to hubby J. Carney.
Behind me, Barnett's Braver, who'll never invite me to tea.
A lonely computer nerd I may be.
But I have credentials, Members of the Academy.
I started in the Gifte Shoppe, I'm family.
I sold brother Roger Evening Shade sweats, don't you see.
I remind Clinton of this some time later as we,
Board an AA plane at LAX en route to IAD,
outside our nation's capital. A bomb had dropped on DC.
A scandal was brewing. Started by me.
He wasn't in the mood to chat, not he.
A moment of silence in honor of the veterans.
Slumbering Sarah cuts a sleepy fart.
It echoes and reverberates.
Well said. Precisely. Couldn't have put it better myself.

THE NIGHT THE GATES BLEW

"I had a little anxiety the next day, of course, because of the DRUDGE REPORT."
>—Bill Clinton—1:30 pm—08/17/98
>Map Room, White House
>Grand Jury Testimony

"I learned it on the DRUDGE REPORT . . . I cried a lot. I freaked out a lot. I mean, it was just—it was scary . . . it wasn't going to be a good year."
>—Monica Lewinsky—6:18 pm—01/03/00
>CNN Sunset Blvd. Studio—Interview

"This is really boring."
>—Katie Couric—12:20 am—01/01/00
>Times Square, NBC

It comes late in the night.

An urgent e-mail.

A juicy goodie from a source who's been on the money in the past, helping me to pull off a series of world exclusives.

The gist:

A former intern has been having an affair with the love of her life, an older married man who happens to be POTUS. She's been signing in at Casa Blanca to "visit" POTUS's secretary, Betty Currie. POTUS has been sending gifts; she's been sending love letters and confiding in a coworker at DOD. Jones lawyers aware. FLOTUS doesn't have a clue. Intern has been gratifying POTUS with his favorite sexual preference. NYC book agent Lucianne Goldberg knows all. Her phone # is 212-555-5555.

Goldberg? Currie? Favorite sexual preference?

FLOTUS doesn't have a clue?

The tip isn't anything special, I decide. I've received so many, after all. On the secretary who was once a stewardess (also, allegedly into heavy service). On the nanny. On the movie star. On the night Bill Clinton lost his wedding ring. The "cousin," the cousin's cousin, not to mention Miss America. The electric company employee, the judge, the nursing home director. On Sweet Connie, named for a song. Not unlike DOPOTUS Chelsea, about whom I'd also received e's and who was only a couple of years younger than the former Casa La Blanca intern. Am I going too fast?

How to verify any of this? Where to begin?

"Tip on Intern" goes into the Keeps File.

I'm running out of hard drive, there's so much info living there. Besides, I'm working a high-impact POTUS story that is going to rock the crowd:

"Clinton Orders 'Boogie Nights' For White House Theater."

I've been building this all night. I pound out details.
TripHop tracks blast in my headphones, DirecTV Ch #812.

During his latest swing through Los Angeles, President Clinton revealed that he tries to catch as many movies as possible. He told reporters that he uses films to unwind from the stress of his job. Last week he caught L.A. Confidential and he loved it. Now, the Drudge Report can reveal, the President of the United States can't wait to see New Line's Boogie Nights! The president has ordered the raunchy look at the '70s–'80s porn biz for a screening in the White House theater!

'No, I don't imagine Hillary will watch it with him,' a Clinton staffer told the report late tonight.

The White House had no official comment and wouldn't release specific information on a Boogie Nights screening, but the movie's promosite—http://www.boogie-nights.com— promises the president one hell of a ride.

On the movie's lead character, porn-ace Dirk Digler: 'In an industry that goes up and down more than a ferris wheel, Dirk Diggler's talents remain rock solid. He's the winner of over 15 Adult Film Awards and the actor who put act back in the actor. Since 1977, Diggler's been hot and heavy and packing 'em in. He's a consummate professional whose work with Director Jack Horner changed the face of the adult film industry. Horner says, "He's not just a c**k, he's an actor" . . . Horner has made such films as Inside Amber, Amanda's Ride, Angels Live in My City, Oral Majesty, Silver Fingers, Blow by Blow, Rock Harders in Heat, Rock Harders Bi the Book . . .'

I launch the story with a siren on my website.
Spam my e-mail list of about 75,000 addresses, collected over the past 3 years.
Boogie that, Boogie Boy!
In space everyone can hear you scream.
"You've outdone yourself with this one, Mr. D," the executive at New Line who tipped me off to the presidential request over drinks at the Four Seasons laughs to my receptionist, AT&T 1872.

Hit the mailbox at drudgereport.com.

681 messages left to download.

Looks like a smash.

A reporter for NBC News in DC is in the queue: "Drudge, the Lincoln Bedroom is safe! I hear they're showing Boogie Nights at Camp David during Thanksgiving break."

I e back: "Will you report it? Or is your boss Tim Russert going to be there for the screening?"

Grab a shower.

Draining the Hollywood Reservoir, I smile while Irish Springing. I'm no Dirk Diggler, but my Boogie Nights story is built. A classic Drudge: expose the real state of leadership in the country sensationally enough to get coverage all day tomorrow on am/pm AM/FM shortwave/broadband. Ham.

Toweling off I hear Arianna Huffington huffing to my receptionist. It's after midnight. Boy, she's up late.

My movie flash must be taking off.

"She's reporting an FOB who lied about his war record is buried in Arlington Cemetery, Cat yawns. *She's going to get him exhumed."*

What!? Pump up the volume.

"Larrrreeee Lawrence donated over two huuundred t'ousand dollahs to Cleeenton's election campaign, he flew on Air Force One, he was appointed Umbahsssahdor to Sweetzerland, hosted the President at his Corrronado Island estate, and was burrried een Arlington . . ."

"Arianna, hold on! I'm just getting out of the shower."

"That's your third one today."

"Do you vaaant me to call you beck, sveetheart?" Huffington asks politely.

"No, this sounds hot! I thought you were calling about Boogie Nights," I say, standing naked in all my glory.

"Booogie V'aaat?"

"Never mind. How did you find out about this Arlington thing and Larry . . . ?"

"Larrreee Lawrence. His longtime assistant is telling me t'ings. She says he made up his vaaar record. Lahnny Davis is at the White House telling everyone Lawrence vass injured at sea in 1945 v'en the Leeberty ship S.S. Horace Bushnell vass torpedoed by a Cherman sub in the Artic. Can you believe?"

"Arianna, this is huge."

"I know. I'ff given it to the Veteran's Affaaairs subcommeettee. There eeesss no record of him being injured at sea. Vant more? I'm vorking on it rrright now for my column. I gaaafe a sneak preview on Poleetically Eencorrect tonight."

"More news is broken on PI these days than Nightline," I joke, quickly lower the Boogie Nights headline and replace it with "TOMB OF THE VERY UNKNOWN SOLDIER!"

Siren.

I continue jazzing with Huffington for a while.

Type up a story. Post. Spam.

Update AOL Keyword: Drudge.

This has to be my Last Dance.

I have to call it a night.

I notice an e marked high priority.

"I like movies as much as the next guy. But Boogie Nights stars an intern on location at Discotheque Casa Blanca. Repeat. Jones lawyers aware. Repeat. NYC book agent Lucianne Goldberg knows all . . ."

Yeah, right. It also stars the secretary who was once a stewardess, the nanny, the "cousin," the cousin's cousin, Miss America, the electric company employee, the judge, the nursing home director, Sweet Connie, Dirk Diggler and Larry Lawrence. But.

I've really got to get some sleep.

For the next two months, sources descend from Olympus and rise from Hades. They want *in* on the action.

"Exclusive: Judge Rules 'Distinguishing Characteristic' Not Explored."

"Exclusive: Gore Campaign Web Address Registered From White House."

"Exclusive: Paula Jones Case: Intrigue Around Woman Named 'Juanita.' "

"Exclusive: Chelsea Becomes Vegetarian."

Yes, there's suck.com. Yes, there's onion.com. Hotwired. MSNBC. But they're narrowly niched or inefficiently corporate.*[#11]

I continue to be the only individual on the net making a name for himself, and net news is starting to make such an impact—on and off net—I'm asked to appear in all kinds of niched and corporate LegacyMedia outlets, who fall hard for my standard quote:

"I just go where the stink is."

I witness firsthand just how stinky the stink is from the inside.

A photo shoot for a Vanity Fair profile where the mag fudges the credits for my wardrobe.

"Matt Drudge's Ralph Lauren shirt from Ralph Lauren, Beverly Hills. Echo tie from Saks Fifth Avenue stores nationwide."

Actually, the white shirt's thrift shop, and the trademark black tie's The Gap, but Editor E. Graydon Carter apparently doesn't consider them trendy enough.

I keep quiet.

Ha.

An interview for a Nightline profile where images of Nazis are voice-overed by the reporter saying "Drudge." I know the producers for the show have edited them in. But.

I keep quiet.

Ha-ha.

A phone conversation with Columbia Journalism Review Publisher Joan Konner about her quotes in a Page One Christian Science Monitor profile: "Drudge isn't a reporter . . . When I was 16 years old, I was the editor of my camp gossip sheet. Does that make me a journalist?" *[#12]

The professor confesses she's never actually read my report.

I *do not* keep quiet.

Ha-ha-ha.

And by the way, thanks for making me a household name. Class dismissed.

January 17, 1998
2:45 p.m. PT

A slow Saturday afternoon in Hollywood and a layer's already moved into the basin.

I've finished the Boxoffice Report.

Mrs. Doubtfire (The Good Crossdresser) 15,000,000 and Schindler's List (The Good Nazi) 3,700,000 top a mediocre list.

Police Scanner's quiet.

APUPIREUTERSAFP's putting me to sleep.

The Brits have nothing for Sunday Tabs.

It's the fourth anniversary of the Northridge Quake (MLK's Birthday Observed). I finger the CalTechServer. No action. That's good. Some 2.0's up in Baker, home of the world's largest thermometer at BunBoy (not rectal, I swear).

A 3.0 in the Salton Sea.

I check my giant faultline map—strategically hung on one of my 3-room apartment's fading smog-stained walls to conceal cracks caused, in fact, by Northridge. I search for the Salton Sea, outside Palm Springs, where a guest on Art Bell's wildly successful overnight talkshow prophesied that the Big One is coming.

9.0 or greater, said Gordon Michael Scallion.

Any day now.

On the desk in my living room, all three computers are searching for the catch of the day, but no fish.

A country away in DC, Clinton's being deposed.

It should end shortly.

Any day now.

The judge in the Paula Jones Case, Susan Weber Wright (a former student of Professor Clinton) flew to Washington to referee.

He's been in for hours.

Guess it's not going too well.

I go into the kitchen to slap together a peanut butter and honey sandwich. If I'd known this would be the last solid food I'd put into my belly for the next 48 hours, I'd have made at least two.

I grab some carrots and return to the wires.

There it is.

AP NewsAlert's been issued.

Depo Finito.

I throw a siren.

What the hell.

Waitaseconn, what's this?!

Another high priority e from my initial intern tipster:

"It's in play! Intern! Casa Blanca! Goldberg . . . Isikoff . . . Tripp Tapessss! Coming Newsweek! In the morning!"

Ohhhh I remember.

6:30 pm PT

Phone rings. AT&T receptionist grabs it.

"Druuudge, this is Larrrry Nichols. Whaddya know 'bout dat interrrrn!?"

Larry Nichols. Conway, Arkansas.

The original Whitewater Star.

Nichols, whose voice sounds like he's gargled with Ajax, works talkradio like no one works talkradio. He's spent the better part of the nineties chronicling various Clinton misdeeds. His one-man jihad commenced upon his firing from the Arkansas Finance Development Authority for placing hundreds of calls to the Contras, which he claims is a phony charge cooked up by "Arkansas Mafia."

After Nichols was canned, he launched a suit in which he named five women he swore the Arkansas Governor had porked.

Hence, Gennifer Flowers. Hence, the "cousins."

Hence, The Troopers. Paula. Kathleen.

Hence, Linda.

Hence. Hence. Hence.

I could hear from his voice on the phone all the way from Conway that Pitbull Nichols had caught the scent of a woman who was about to become the ultimate scandal.

Goodbye Castle Grande. Goodbye FBI Files.

Travel Office/Vince Foster. Mena. Cattle futures.

Charlie Trie. Buddhist Monks. It's been real.

Hello Intern!

And FLOTUS doesn't have a clue.

What*ever*.

7:18 pm PT

Hollywood. DRUDGE REPORT Newsroom.

Built by Radio Shack.

I sit at the keyboard frantically typing an item that Newsweek's preparing to unload and unload big. My inside source confirms that Michael Isikoff's heard tapes, but once again—as I did by six weeks with his Willey—I'm beating him to the punchbowl.

I've gotta get hold of Isikoff before unleashing.

I don't have his number. I check switchboard.com, which databases the home numbers/addresses of everyone—listed and un.

Ken Starr. Maureen Dowd. Brian Lamb. Janet Reno.

David Brock. Michael Isikoff. There it is.

"Hello," says a vibrant female voice.

"Is Mike there?"

"Yes, he is. Whom shall I say is calling?"

"It's Matt Drudge."

"I-I-I-I'm sorry," she stutters suddenly, in a stricken whisper. Pause. Busted. "He's asleep right now," she adds without much conviction and hangs up quickly.

I'm minutes—make that *seconds*—away from slapping a screamer on my website: NEWSWEEK BOMBSHELL: TAPES REVEAL INTERN IN WHITE HOUSE SEX SHOCKER; PREZ GAVE GIFTS; STARR MOVES IN!!!

Hold on.

I should call NYC book agent Lucianne Goldberg.

Who knows all, according to my original e, I recall.

"Tip on Intern" out of Keeps File.

212-555-5555.

"Hellooooo . . ."

"Lucianne Goldberg? This is Matt Drudge from Holly-wood . . ."

"Oh, hi, dear."

"I run a website called the DRUDGE REPORT . . ."

"I know, dear, I was on it earlier this evening . . ."

"Oh, really? How wonderful . . ."

"Indeed, dear . . ."

"Listen, I know the hour's late, but can I ask you a few questions?"

"Yeah, what's up? Hold on, hold on . . . let me move into my office. My husband's sleeping . . ."

Cat, slumbering soundly in a corner, wakes up just long enough to shoot me a disdainful look.

"Working on those life-or-death Friday night boxoffice stats again, Drudge? More synthespians in hotsy films?"

"I'm back, dear. [Click] Whatcha got? [Clink]"

"I hear NEWSWEEK is about to bust an intern who's having sex with Clinton."

"No, they spiked the story."

_____

7:45 pm PT

_____

"Whaaaat? They killed the story? What happened?"

"I don't know what happened. I'm devastated . . ."

"I was just about to post a headline. I'm so glad I reached you."

"Yeah, Newsweek chickened out . . ."

"Did Katherine Graham kill it?"

"Who knows? Probably . . ."

"Was Linda Tripp really taping the intern?"

"Her name is Monica, dear. Monica Lewinsky. She lives in the Watergate."

_____

8:01pm PT

_____

My new best friend Goldberg and I rattle on; she drops more details.

I quietly type a new headline:

NEWSWEEK KILLS STORY ON WHITE HOUSE INTERN X X X X BLOCKBUSTER REPORT: 23-YEAR-OLD, FORMER WHITE HOUSE INTERN, SEX RELATIONSHIP WITH PRESIDENT!!!

What am I doing here? Do I really wanna do this? Does this woman know what she's talking about? If it's wrong, I'm finished.

De-listed from the Entertainment Section on Yahoo!.

Banished for*ever* to HoaxKooks and ConspiracyLoserListings.

Back to the Gifte Shoppe, with a couple of souvenirs.

"Lemme fax you her resume, dear."

"You have her resume?"

"Yeah, and get this. She's got top secret clearance to the Pentagon."

She has the resume. She has the goods.

My palms begin to sweat.

"I gotta jump, Lucianne Goldberg. I gotta do this. I gotta expose how NEWSWEEK is scared to report this . . ."

"I've been working on it for months. Ah, hell, type up some copy and call me right back?"

"How do you spell her last name?"

"Lewinsky. L-E-W-I-N-S-K-Y . . . Bye [Click]." Click.

Click.

Hot! I gotta take a shower.

Fade Out. Fade Up.

After jamming a chair under my front door and donning my favorite boxers-not-briefs, I settle down.

My fingers fly across the Packard Bell keyboard without me:

At the last minute, at 6 pm Saturday evening, NEWS-WEEK magazine killed a story that was destined to shake official Washington to its foundation . . .

Words spill across the screen before I think them:

The DRUDGE REPORT has learned that reporter Michael Isikoff developed the story of his career, only to have it spiked by top NEWSWEEK suits hours before publication. A young woman, 23 . . . wrote long love letters to President Clinton, which she delivered through a delivery service. She was a frequent visitor at the White House after midnight, where she checked in the WAVE logs as visiting a secretary named Betty Currie, 57 . . . tapes of intimate phone conversations exist . . .

I'm flowing like Niagara Falls.

NEWSWEEK and Isikoff were planning to name the woman. Word of the story's impending release caused blind chaos in media circles; TIME magazine spent Saturday scrambling for its own version of the story. The NEW

YORK POST on Sunday was set to front the young intern's affair, but . . .

I'm at the top of Mount Everest!

The story was set to break just hours after President Clinton testified in the Paula Jones sexual harassment case . . . Isikoff was not available for comment late Saturday. NEWSWEEK was on voice mail.

The White House was busy checking the DRUDGE REPORT for details.

I'm the Earl of url.
No, I'm King of the Ftp*ing World!
Written. Spellchecked. Done.
Goldberg confirms [Click]. Click. Click.

9:02 pm PT

Nothing left to do.
My finger's poised over the button.
This is everything.
Everything you've ever been and everything you'll ever be . . .
"Whaddya think yer doin', Drudge . . ."
Cat. Bummer.
"Am I reading this right? You're about to accuse POTUS of having it off with an intern? Are you preparing to blow up Washington? Get me Janet Reno . . . !"
"Hey, I don't like it either, but it's confirmed confirmed confirmed, and your Janet Reno's authorized Starr to move in . . ."
"You are a terrorist, aren't you?"
"Mommy and Daddy were liberals . . ."
"You and your internet manifesto."
"Let the future begin . . ."
"So be it . . ."
Microsoft mouse moved into position.

Ready. Aim. ENTER.
"What's done is done."
"What's done is done."
What's done is done . . .

Bouncing beams from dish to dish, e's, faxes & alarms. 1 am.
Cellphones, conference calls, dirty dresses, cigars. 2 am.
Subpoenas. Grand Juries. Fallout. 3 am.
Elections. Impeachment. 4 am.
Acquittal. 5 am.
Fame. 6 am.
Dawn.

January 18, 1998
8:00 am PT

Fully expecting the LAPD to batter-ram my apartment door on some false pretext or other (too much police-scanner scanning), I've stayed barricaded in.

I haven't slept a wink.

I've received over 15,000 e-mails and it's only eight hours into the cycle. I monitor the East Coast feed on DirecTV nervously.

No mention on Meet The Press. /zap.

No mention on Face the Nation. \zap.

No callers into Washington Journal.

/zap \zap /zap

Oh, well.

ABC's This Week—chaotic since Brinkley's departure—is in progress.

Kristol: "The story in Washington this morning is that News-week magazine was going to go with a big story based on tape-recorded conversations, which a woman who was a summer intern at the White House—"

Stephanopoulos: "And, Bill, where did it come from? The Drudge Report. You know we've all seen how discredited—"

Kristol: "No no no they had screaming arguments at News-week yesterday. They finally didn't go with the story. It's going to be a question of whether the media is now going to report what are pretty well validated charges . . ."

Donaldson: "I'm not an apologist for Newsweek . . . but I don't think we can say Newsweek was wrong to kill it—"

Cokie: "There was another piece of news this week, believe it or not. This time, the Republicans seem to have gotten out from under a difficult fight for them. Or maybe not."

Aaahhh, Cokie's nose for news. Resolutely on message, obliging the networks' blackouts on my reports, filled as they are with pregnant possibilities.

Notwithstanding pressure from Ken Starr's office to slow down via goo-goo e's from an MSNBC faux anchor, for four long days, I'm the lonely only reporting Lewinsky anything and everything.

The Big Boys let me swing gently in the wind, until January 21, when the Washington Post finally breaks water.

In the meantime, the Drudge Report is hopping and the story keeps on popping. Above the fold. Wait. There isn't a fold.

Because the story remains web-exclusive. LegacyMedia continues its blackout, but thanks to ABC's brief churlish Sunday-Morning mention, inside sources find me:

The Lewinsky Friend.

The White House Staffer.

The Case Lawyer.

The Tripp Relative.

They can't wait to talk.

Apparently, I'm the only one listening.

Within 24 hours, I issue three updates.

10:09 pm PT

I slap Lewinsky's resume on my site.

Two minutes after I post/siren/spam I check free republic.com, a new-wave bulletin board composed of headlines and instant reactions.

There's a party in progress. The Freepers are going wild.

Amcon1: I wonder how diligently this computer literate psych major was vetted by the FBI or DOD in securing a top secret clearance?

Waco: The boy on the web has the mainstream press on their knees.

Trailertrash: Heck of a story. Wonder if it'll grow legs.

D-Boy: Prediction: settlement w/ Paula Jones by Friday [after deadlines] much embarrassment more spin. Press will consider this a non-issue by the following Tuesday. End of story. Case closed.

D-Boy is D-Wrong.

January 19, 1998
1:54 am PT

Sleepless Night II

Carmen McCrae basso-profundos Send in the Clowns; Shirley Horn sings the longest, slowest version of My Funny Valentine.

Erik Satie's Gymnopedies.

I PostSpamSiren: "Former White House Intern Denies Sex With President In Sworn Affadavit."

The sun is rising in London.*[#13]

From an unimpeachable Insider, I've procured the document, which, it would be learned, was roughed-out in something called The Talking Points, discovered on the hard drive of TS-SCI, the woman of easy virtue with Pentagon clearance.

Ironically, the affidavit had been filed just in time for the President's deposition, which ended a mere 90 minutes before Cat and I agreed I should hit ENTER.

Back to The Freepers:

GoBillGo: Maybe Isikoff and Newsweek set up Drudge for another lawsuit. Wag the Dog.

Dogfight: Is Drudge failing us or what? Now, whatever he says will be laughed at by the lib press. The White House must be so happy tonight.

MsLady: How do we know Drudge put this headline up? Maybe he was hacked.

MsLady is misguided. *I* do the hacking in this newsroom!

3:07 am PT

The sun is rising in Manhattan.

"Hey, dear. Great posts this morning. Glad you got the resume in. You know, Starr's asked Justice for permission to move in. He's looking at perjury charges," sayeth LucianneGoldberg NYCBookAgentWhoKnowsAll. [Click]

"So I hear. Is anyone else going to jump in?"

"I don't know, honey. Even the guys at the New York Post are afraid of this one. I'd watch Sue Schmidt at the Washington Post though. She's champing at the bit."

"Oh, Kay Graham's loosening up?"

"Who knows? Possibly . . ."

"I called her yesterday to ask if she put the brakes on Newsweek, but like a good journalist, she wouldn't come to the phone."

"That's cute."

"I hear NBC's got a copy of her denial affadavit."

"Yeah, Bennett's probably spreading it around . . ."

"David Bloom asked some of the PJ lawyers for comment, so I called him for a comment on his attempt to get a comment. He freaked."

"Yeah, he's a real jerk. Could you hold off on the Starr info, darling, 'til I get back to you?"

The story is so sordid, I feel the need to stay ultraclean.

I consider taking my keyboard into the shower with me.

Any time now, the sun will be rising in Los Angeles.

1:19 pm ET/DC

In the capital, the sun is up and so is Sam's dander.

It's his first day back on the White House beat.

GersteinShipmanBlitzerBloomThomasBraverHunt give him room to rove during his inaugural White House Press Briefing.

Donaldson: Someone said that you have put out the word that staffers at the The White House should not be allowed to log on to the DRUDGE REPORT. Is that true?

McCurry: I—I don't discuss that subject.

Donaldson: What? Whether you have put out the word that you can't log on?

McCurry: I've heard calling it a report is too generous.

Laughter.

Donaldson: Well, whatever you want to call it is fine with me, but have you forbidden people to actually log on to the DRUDGE REPORT?

McCurry: It's a free country, and people do what they want to on the internet.

Sam doesn't mention L-E-W-I-N-S-K-Y, but behind the scenes, chaos. Nobody dares state that McCurry's and Currie's boss is in a fight for his life, and White House staffers are reloading and refreshing the DRUDGE REPORT as fast as the circuits allow. Over 6,000 visits from the eop.gov domain in the last 39 hrs.

The main press tries desperately to hold the center.

TIME magazine has just hit the racks in all its glory with an "in-depth insider" dispatch:

"The president felt the deposition had gone smashingly for him."

TIME, the top brand name in J-World, continues:

"Describing the mood Saturday night at the White House, one person close to the President said, 'Everyone is going to sleep well tonight.' Clinton prepared to do just that, forgoing an evening at the Kennedy Center or dinner with Chief of Staff Erskine Bowles to stay in for the night."

TIME mag flacks who contributed to the hot flash, Jay-BranneganMargaretCarlsonMichaelDuffyVivecaNovak, would become a favorite punchline in internet J-classes for years to come.

*   *   *

Months later, having escaped a Vanity Fair party at the Russian Trade Legation for a zigzag walk along Connecticut Avenue, TIME chief Walter Isaacson confessed, "I just use what they give me." My travel partner, Goldberg, NYC book agent who knows all, roared, "I knew you were in bed [clink] with the White House." [click]

Even though TIME told the world the Jones depo had "gone smashingly," Grand Jury Testimony would later prove it had gone crashingly.

And screaming media skunks would spend the next eighteen months obsessively sorting it out, spiking ratings and goosing circulations back to prefade heights.

True. The President didn't go to the Kennedy Center.

True. The President didn't have dinner with Chief of Staff Bowles.

True. The President stayed in.

False. The President did not sleep well.

The President was a very busy boy that night.

Coaching CurrienotCurry, committing acts that would later lead to a serious spanking:

An impeachment count.

What's done is done.

And cannot be undone.

[FILE]

Map Room, White House
August 17, 1998—1:30 pm ET
Grand Jury Grilling

Q: . . . You did have a great deal of anxiety in the hours—following the end of your deposition. Isn't that fair to say?

A: Well, I had a little anxiety the next day, of course, because of the DRUDGE REPORT. And I had an anxiety after the deposition because it was more about Monica Lewinsky than it was Paula Jones . . . this DRUDGE REPORT came out which used Betty's name, and I thought we were going to be deluged by press comments.

Q: Mr. President, when did you learn about the DRUDGE RE-PORT allegations of you having a sexual relationship with someone at the White House?

A: I believe it was the morning of the 18th I think.

Q: What time of day, sir.

A: I have no idea . . . I think somebody called me and told me about it, maybe Bruce. Maybe someone else. I'm not sure, but I learned early on the 18th of the DRUDGE REPORT.

Q: Very early morning hours, sir . . . ?

A: I think it was when I got up Sunday morning, I think. Maybe it was late Saturday night, I don't remember.

Q: Did you call Betty Currie, sir, after the DRUDGE REPORT hit the wire?

A: I did.

Q: Did you call her at home?

A: I did. Was that the night of the 17th?

Q: Night of the 17th . . .

A: Okay, yes, yes. I worked with Prime Minister Netanyahu that night until about midnight . . .

Toda Rabba.

I remember that night.

It was the night the gates blew open.

For news was no longer controlled, and never would be again.

Any*one* from any*where* can cover any*thing*.

And send it out to *everyone*.

Even this nobody. Filing.

From nowhere.

"You've just broken the biggest story in twenty years," my favorite Postie, Howard Kurtz, exclaimed, seeking comment, but of course, I didn't see my name in his colleague Sue Schmidt's blockbuster copy.*[#14]

Sam Donaldson, who originally defended Newsweek's kill, called, somewhat abashed.

"What a treat for my first week back. Thanks."

I take him at his word.

"Don't thank me, Sam, thank the internet."

* * *

I'm sleep-deprived and hungry, as I've been barricaded in my apartment/newsroom for five intensely hectic days.

Living in every time zone, communicating multi-continentally.

AT&T 1872 two-line digital maxed out.

Mailbox at drudgereport.com overloaded and corrupted.

I check my look in the mirror, I need a haircut.

"I need some Sheba!"

"I need to get out."

Sharp right off Franklin. Zoom down the hill at Yucca.

Pass Capitol Records. Punch in Rod McKuen.

The McKuen Greats. Studied every one. Lived some, too.

I've Been To Town. Alone. Seasons in the Sun.

I twitch at the bank on the southwest corner where I deposit my fives and tens. Past Sunset Santa Monica Melrose.

"I need a 39-cent taco, if only to remind myself of who I am!"

Seasons. Fun. Sun.

Rod replies: "But the stars we could reach . . ."

Were just STARRfish on the beach

Well put. Precisely. Couldn't have said it better myself.

Roger Clinton and I whiz across the fruited plains on AA to IAD. He's racing to his brother's side. I'm racing to Tim Russert's.

I'm in Business.

Roger's in First, but I see through the curtain he's reading the LAT we'd both picked up at LAX.

Over and over, trancing on the front-page scandal story.

Mischief-making, I phone CNN's Lucy Spiegel, the best Legacy-Media producer in Washington.

"Hey, Lucy, it's Drudge, calling from thirty-thousand feet."

"Where are you?"

"Lemme look . . . Austin, I think, over some bushes."

"You gonna make it in time for Reliable? We go live at six."

"Yeah, I hope so. Can't wait to get it on with Kalb. Will he be alive at six?" Lucy doesn't know if she should laugh or not, so I press on. "I just wanted to give you a heads-up that Roger Clinton is on the plane with me—AA to IAD."

"You and Roger on the same plane? I'll have cameras waiting. Hope you took out some insurance . . ."

The stews have finished their "welcome to IAD thanks for flying AA" riff, and Roger and I deplane.

He dashes into a waiting car on the tarmac.

I race through the terminal, chased by cameras.

Outrun a CNN crew. Jump into a CNN car. Phone Lucy.

"Spiegel, I'll be there in twenty."

"Hurry, Drudge, we go live at six." Phone Lucy.

"Goldberg, have they found the dress yet? Turn on the TV. I'm live at six. On Sources. [click]"

This . . . is CNN. *[#15]

I'm next to Safire, across from Isikoff, next to Russert.

Ignoring Stuart Taylor.

This will be the highest-rated MEET THE PRESS since the Gulf War. I try not to take it personally.

"Tim, this intern relationship didn't happen last week; it happened over the course of a year and a half," I remind Russert. "I'm concerned there's a press corps that wasn't monitoring the situation closely enough!"

I like to live in the moment, but I'm still preoccupied with my previous Peacock experience, three days ago.

A continent away in Burbank. 4 am PT.

I was tailed by an unmarked car with tinted windows on a deserted 101 Freeway. North. I was spooked, since it followed me at high speed from my Hollywood newsroom nearly to NBC's.

I outran it in my trusty Metro. Geo Power!

Seemed like a lot to go through just to guest on TODAY.

"You say Monica Lewinsky has a piece of clothing that might have the president's semen on it?" Matt Lauer inquires pugnaciously via satellite.

"Yes, I have reported there is a potential DNA trail that would tie Clinton to this young woman." Starr's office is furious with me for spilling details of the dress.

Two days later, Miz Jackie Judd will take full credit for the break.

And accept a few awards for it.

I know, because I was sitting at a table at the TVandRadio Correspondents Dinner 99.

Sucking on a lemon, I applauded as she made her way to the podium.

Applauding along with me: David Westin (ABC), next to Barbara Walters (ABC), who was trying to charm Champagne Charlie Spencer, who waved to Cheryl Mills, who avoided meeting Bruce Lindsay's eyes too often.

Miz Judd's ABC Producer, Chris Vlasto, found my table.

"You know the dirty dress was my story," I reminded him.

"Oh, whaddya mean, the TODAY show thing?"

"No, I mean the internet. I-N-T-E-R-N-E-T. That's where the story first appeared."

"Oh, thaaat." Chris smiled dismissively and moved on to the next photo-op.

I applauded Michael Isikoff, too, at the White House Correspondents Dinner 99 a few weeks later.

Same room. Same people. Same story.

Same old. Same old.

Applauding along with me: Alan Greenspan, advised by Claire Danes. Ben Bradley, directed by Ron Howard. SeanPenn, JamieRubin, SteveCase, MrMadeleineAlbright&MsAlexanderHaig. Excuse me, MsMr.

Susan McDougal sat on Larry Flynt's lap. Dancing, if you please, while toasting John Kennedy, Jr. Val Kilmer and Colin Powell politely laughed at MC and sometime NewsAnchor Brian Williams(NBC) who was rocked by Aretha Franklin who racked Bill Clinton who avoided meeting Mondale's eyes during "Chain of Fools." Eleanor not Fritz. Jack Valenti gave standing ovation to Melanie Griffith, after chatting up Buckley not Buchwald, William not Art. . . .

"More emotional, get more emotional," urged TODAY Show Executive Producer Jeff Zucker into my IFB, distracting me.

Lauer: So when you write, is it journalism or is it gossip?

Drudge: It's a reporter, not overly educated, not underly educated."*[#16]

Lauer: But are the facts checked and double-checked as you would in journalism, or do you take what you hear and just put it out there?

Drudge: Oh, you mean like Richard Jewell?

Lauer: Yeah, like anything.

Drudge: I guess Richard Jewell was double-checked . . .

NBC's settlement on Richard Jewell's suit was for an undisclosed six-figure amount, I'd read in The Wall Street Journal. Maybe Lauer doesn't have time to check and double-check the paper—the facts—although he is an early riser.

But are they, in fact, the facts?

'Cause didn't The Wall Street Journal lose a record libel case in Texas? $222,000,000.00 worth of jury to choke on? (Later dissolved at the appeal level when litigants found resources were sucked dry by Dow Jones.)

I heard that from Bernie Shaw at CNN. But wait.

Didn't CNN also settle with Jewell?

I learned that in The Weekly Standard. Should I believe it?

Because the same Weekly Standard was sued by Deepak Chopra for libel/defamation and had to settle bigtime.

I read about that on Salon.com.

Don't download just yet!

Salon's top reporter was Jonathan Broder, who was fired from the Chicago Tribune for plagiarism. According to the Weekly Standard. As reported on CNN.

This is definite material for an exhaustive in-depth New Republic profile.

Welllll . . . maybe not.

Didn't their Glass get smashed for fabrication?

And then there's Maureen, belle lettrist to the apparatchiki.

Who took "Liberties" with Tom Selleck.

In a letter published by her paper, an aggrieved Magnum P.I. responded: "How sad it is that Maureen Dowd seems so consumed with creating heat at the expense of shedding light. For the record, her August 20 column is erroneous. It is made up of the kind of half-truths and speculation that people assume are the province only of supermarket tabloids. For the record, I have never in my life had a serious conversation about running for public office, and I believe Ms. Dowd did not make a serious effort to call me."

Dowd, who once cadged a NYT front-page piece—referencing none other than Kitty Kelly, belle lettrist to the hoi polloi—by repeating gossip, rumors of a purported affair between Nancy Reagan and Frank Sinatra. Said purported affair "could add allegations of scandalous sexual behavior to the folklore of the Reagan era," Dowd wrote Sunday, April 7, 1991.

Dowd finally hit Quindlen Quality—according to Columbia—when she won a Pulitzer last century, reworking Linda Tripp's material.

Mirror mirror on the wall.

To replace her, Anna Quindlen touted Dowd, after all.

The Ronde de le Monde . . .

I could get real emotional about the state of the union, Zucker, but I don't think Sir Safire will approve. Not on national TeeVee.

"It's your time, son. Enjoy it," the NYT star says condescendingly as he wipes off his MEET THE PRESS makeup, waves goodbye, and turns right on Nebraska.

LA RONDE DE LE MONDE 2000

Reporters marry sources who work for clients who employ bureau chiefs
Who dine with agents who wine the lawyers who date the editors
Who have sex with the reporters who share the beachhouses
With the sources who are married to the bureau chiefs
Who hire the reporters who are married
To the lawyers who date
The columnists
That dish
Stars
Who dine
With the editors
Who have sex with
The sources after meeting
With lawyers who lobby Congress
To protect a president who is friends with
The bureau chiefs who hire the reporters who
Have sex with the editors who blast the internet websites . . .

The reporters the editors the bureau chiefs the columnists the lobbyists the agents of the lawyers of the presidents who share beachhouses with the ghosts of Kennedy JohnSrJr who had sex with MarilynMadonna who lost heavy rotation to MarilynnotCharlieManson whose HowardRush publisher RegannotReagan signed Noonan who dated Jeff before Rick seduced him with mixed results from ABC to CNN which was started by Ted who married JaneFonda not Peter with mixed results after hiring Christiane who married Jamie after dating Jr whose ghost shares the beachhouse with the president who ordered The War covered by Christiane after daily debriefing by Jamie who speaks for Madeline who watched Susan lapdance Larry who lobbied the president who dated Miss America who was hired by HarrynotLinda ThomasonnotBloodworth who transformed Hillary who gave birth to Chelsea who bought a T-shirt from Matt DrudgenotLauer before going to Stanford with Starr whose father subpoenaed Sidney whose best friend James married Mary who managed George Sr not Jr before co-hosting with DeeDee who wrote for Vanity not George founded by Jr not Sr before marrying Todd who writes about James and dines with Sidney who leaks to Jill and Jane who tells husband Bill who edits the story stolen from Todd leaked by Sidney who whispered to Jill who complains to Maureen who ran to Alessandra after being jilted by Michael for Catherine who costarred with Connery who brought ART to the world . . . Catherine wore Karan not Lauren. Michael wore Calvin not Todd.

Oldham not Purdum reported Lloyd who's always with Kim (who shies away from Karen) but shares the style section with Sally (who can). Donna designs suits for Sally's husband Ben who edits Lloyd who reports to Katherine who brought down Dick thanks to Ben's Bob and Carl whose ex-wife Nora was played by Meryl who won an Oscar because of Sydney not Sidney and wears Klein not Karan whose best friend Barbra not Barbara married James. Brolin not Carville. The Way We Are Now. Lyrics: Bergmans. Music: Hamlisch. Laura who kissed Jim not Warren who shares the op-ed section with Bob not Roland EvansnotEmmerich who watches Dave who hates Jay who is hated by Bill who hangs out with Hefner thanks to Brillstein not Brill after courting TV not Court TV which is owned by Ted who competes with C-SPAN as reported by Army who served in the Navy with George and John Sr not Jr who died in the ocean next to the beachhouse which knocked Diana off heavy rotation sang Marilyn. Manson not Monroe. Impacting on MTV VH-1 and MTV2 which were replaced by MUCH carried by TCI which was replaced by DirecTV using synchronous satellite orbiting envisioned by Arthur C. Clarke whose movies play on HBO 1 2 and 3 which is owned by Ted who is owned by Steve who cleaved to Gerald who reports only to God who created All . . . and is so sorry he did . . .

This is too cool for school!
This is not Russert. *This* is *not* CNN.
Not Lauer. Not Letterman.
I'm in control of the mike.
Red light. Out of national news six minutes past the hour.
Engineer waves.
Clear throat. Swallow.
Tilt hat. Yeah, like that.
Live at 50,000 watts.

"I'm Matt Drudge, somewhere in New York City," I begin. "One of the first guys to make a name for himself on the internet, showing my voice on radio."

Dim lights. Cue music. Barbra Streisand. Singing Sondheim.
Children Will Listen from Into the Woods.

"Barbara Streisand, where are you now!" I belt out to *my* audience. "News that Hollywood producer Harry Thomason is once again en route to Washington, DC—this time to help President Clinton prepare for his grand jury testimony—took me back to a more innocent time. Back to the beginning. Back to another cold day in Washington: Inauguration Eve, 1993. And another Harry Thomason production.

"Some eighteen thousand guests had gathered at Washington's Capital Center for the fifty-second Inaugural Gala: 'An American Reunion.'

"It was aired on CBS-TV. It was Michael Jackson and Fleetwood Mac, wishing the new President well. It was La Streisand. Dressed in a white Donna Karan that was cut down to here and slashed up to there, with a face that celebrated the end of Reagan and Bush slavery. Streisand was in top form that night. She belted out a jazzy version of God Bless America—caressing the word 'sweet.' She sang Evergreen and dedicated it to lovebirds Bill and Hillary Clinton—sitting just a few rows up.

"CBS cameras, with Harry Thomason's direction, captured Hillary looking out at the seats, out at the future with love and wonder. Everything was right on that magical DC night . . .

"But it was Streisand's third musical selection that would end up turning into a presidential prophecy.

"Just hours before Bill Clinton was sworn in, there was Streisand on stage, before a national audience, lecturing Clinton to be careful: children are listening.

"It is not clear if Harry Thomason personally approved her playlist.

"Streisand, sitting on a stool, looking directly at Bill Clinton, sipped her tea, flipped her hair, opened her heart and sang.

"The camera caught Bill Clinton misting up during the serenade.

"Hillary nodded with approval as Streisand warned about the perils of lying.

"Because children listen. And learn.

"She sang:

" 'Careful the tale you tell.'

"Streisand hit the high notes flawlessly. The crowd cheered.

" 'Careful before you say: Listen to me.'

"The crowd went wild. Streisand blew kiss, flipped hair, sipped tea.

"Of course, no one in the arena that night could have any idea that Bill Clinton would later appear before a federal grand jury to face questions about what he did as he watched a White House intern do strange things with his *cigars* in the Oval Office.

"Children, run for cover!

"I'm Matt Drudge on NewsTalk 770 WABC."

This is the first cigar reference to appear anywhere.
Finally! I've popped a story too hot to be co-opted.
*My*self, *my* way, on a giant LegacyMedia outlet!
ABC's flagship station!
Eat your heart out, Miz Jackie Judd.

A few years later, in a desperate attempt to sell albums, and after complaining vociferously about the press and stalkarazzi invading her private life, Barbra Streisand conveys her intimate wedding photos to People magazine. Her 1999 album, A Love Like Ours, also featuring candid shots of Streisand and hubby James Brolin, peaks at number six on Billboard and tops out single platinum.

A week later, I fill in cigar details on the I-N-T-E-R-N-E-T:

XXX DRUDGE REPORT XXX
AUGUST 22, 1998 13:20 ET XXX

SHOCK REPORT: SHE HAD SEX WITH CIGAR!

XXX DRUDGE REPORT XXX
AUGUST 22, 1998 14:27 ETXXX

MEDIA STRUGGLES WITH SHOCKING NEW DETAILS OF WHITE HOUSE AFFAIR!
Warning: contains graphic description
In a bizarre daytime sex session that occurred just off the Oval Office in the White House, President Clinton watched as intern Monica Lewinsky masturbated with his cigar.

It has been learned that several major news organizations have confirmed the shocking episode and are now struggling to find ways to report the full Lewinsky/Clinton grossout.

According to multiple sources close to the case, Clinton masturbated as Lewinsky performed the sex show with his cigar. It is not clear if Lewinsky testified on the specifics of the encounter before a federal grand jury this week but the president has.

The DRUDGE REPORT has now been briefed on these shocking details that have stunned all those who have heard them and investigated them—details which now threaten to completely disgust and stun the American electorate.

The White House refuses to comment on any DRUDGE REPORT.

XXX

I'm not much for bowling, but I've hit a strike.
Monday AM, sanitized versions of Cigar hit The Trifecta: LimbaughImusStern©.
By the afternoon:
LiddyPutnamGrantHannityElderCarrSavageHendrie©.
JayLenoOpeningMonologue© before bed . . .
. . . LondonPapers™ after nap.
I'm King of the Ftp*ing World!

"Well, look who's here . . . I let you go to New York and you turn into Larry Flynt. Proud of yourself, Drudge? Like, really, masturbation stories?"
Cat's concept of "Welcome Home from the front lines."
"Jeez, it stinks in here," I say meanly.
"You know, I count on you to clean my litter box, too, not just Washington's . . ."
I can't resist checking out Lexis Nexis.
Drudge: 193 mentions in the past week.
Hmmm . . .
ChrisVlasto: 2. Mr. Oh thaaaat.
Referring to the internet.
Bet he's learned how to spell it by now.
Because in a hair over six months the net has become *the* peristolsis regulating the gut of The24/7Beast (PatentPending).
Investigate the facts. Deliver the news. Set the agenda.
No editor no lawyer no judge no president . . .
Their future has become my past.
While they're fiddling with uplinks and downlinks, I've turned my website into the ultimate pop one-stop shop: The best columnists, best wire services, best weather links and earthquake twinks.
Quickload. Clutter-free. Simple as the pamphleteers.
Presented in plain black and white and read all over.*[#17].

Lawsuit/Linda/Lewinsky turns out to be a major career boost.
The random ReutersFlash© begets CNNHeadlineNews™ begets UPISpotlight® begets RushLimbaugh©. The Flash© becomes A Story after 157 minutes. It begets VanityFairTimeEntertainmentTonightCapitalGang[sm]. It lasts three and one-quarter days and

runs below the fold WeekinReviewNewYorkTimes© and above in EntertainmentLastWeekly©. Two weeks, and someone at US-NewsAndWorld® pounds a WashingtonWhisper©. A month, and RandomHouseReganBooksDoubleday™ approach. BarryKemp pitches an "internet reporter" character to Paramount just as DavidE.Kelley© demanding Emmy, races a secret script for a series starring LeanNLovelyLollipops (PatentPending). Still bouncing in six months, NightlineSpecial© that began . . . with the stray ReutersFlash© a thousand cycles ago. But. A thousand isn't a million.

And a million isn't what it used to be.

"Matt Drudge, who is moderately well known, may, over the course of the next few weeks become very well known, because he is being sued for libel by a White House aide," Nightline host Koppel introduced.

"January 8, 1998, 11:35 pm Eastern Time on the ABC Television Network—the meatball—which was the dreamchild of Goldenson, who engineered the ABC/CapCities merger in '85. Also mentor to Diller and Eisner, who owns and operates ABC, with mixed results," Cat says. *"And Mr. Koppel and his hair were right! 'Over the course of the next few weeks' you did get very well known when we let loose on Lewinsky. January 17, 1998, 10:45 pm Eastern Time. The night the gates blew open, as I call it . . ."*

"Credit-grabber. When did you go so Hollywood?"

"When I moved in with you . . ."

"Just remember, Cat, Goldenson died all alone in Florida, leaving his animals to fend for themselves . . ."

"Hey, that's showbiz."

To David Letterman: " 'I don't care what they say as long as they keep suing,' Winchell used to say."

More orange than Murdoch. St. Bart's or are you an Erno Lazlo Evening?

CBS, Ed Sullivan Theater.

To bodyguards: "Do we really need to go through the kitchen to get out?"

Mosh pit of autograph seekers. Applause.

National Press Club.

To Congressmen: "Your constituents know everything you know and possibly more."

Why isn't C-SPAN around when you want them?

Capitol Hill, Drudge Address #3 to lawmakers about the access edit headline linking of it all.

To Senator Fred Thompson: "I want to show you this tape . . ."

They're not gonna do anything about Waco. They're just curious . . .

Hotel room in Colorado with Chairman Burton and Thompson.

To Jeopardy: "Thank you."

But no thank you.

Celebrity Jeopardy Invite.

From Jeopardy: "The online report known for its sludge . . ."

For $200, Alex. Who is Drudge?

Jeopardy Question.

To photographer: "Okay, fine, I'll drop my pants and hold the laptop."

Time Warner's current concept of photojournalism.

People mag—25 Most Intriguing of the Year, last year.

Early March—Late-'90s—Midnight
Washington, DC

I'm marking time between missions in a junior suite at the Marriott Hotel off M. I'm wide awake and restless: no earthquake alerts issued by EDIS, no tornado warnings issued by NWS, no tsunamis, no subpoenas issued by EOP or DOJ.

How to fill this in-between? Maybe some mischief?

Armed with a fresh cosmopolitan and the latest Baloney Boulevard bunk (test-screening results of a BigSummerPicture from ParamountDreamWorks) I decide to have some fun with my readers and amuse myself.

I throw up a headline with a siren and offer no backup.

XXX DRUDGE REPORT XXX
MARCH 10, 1998 22:02 EST XXX

MSNBC: ASTEROID STREAKING TOWARDS EARTH!

XXX

Panicky e-mail pours in immediately.

FreeRepublic.com threads start within minutes.

"I've had the TV on all night, how did I miss this?" posts clinton-isatraitor.

"Should I be moving into my bomb shelter?" queries treason-isthereason.

I let the headline hang for a half hour.

Take a couple of sips and pop some joints over my Fujitsu-Lifebook©.

10:48 pm ET

"There are late reports tonight," I write, "that a massive aster-oid is believed to be on a direct collision course with planet Earth!"

Another sip. Siren still spinning, I continue my teaser:

"MSNBC is reporting exclusively that the U.S. Government has been secretly preparing for a possible asteroid/Earth colli-sion for more than a year.

"Stunned viewers were instructed not to be alarmed: there is a course of action well under way inside the highest offices of the land."

Slurp! This is fun!

"The Pentagon has been secretly planning a joint venture with Russian military officials, MSNBC revealed, with plans to transport a team of multinational experts via space shuttle and space station to the asteroid.

"The team will drill large holes into it, fill them with nuclear warheads and detonate the asteroid before it can reach Earth."

I jump up briefly for a refill. Return to my newsroom.

AT&TWorldNet connection established.

Finger ready, perfectly positioned.

Eudora loaded. FTP cranked.

Do I really wanna do this? Of course I do.

ENTER.

Readers will soon realize I'm finking a film!

"A massive asteroid is believed to be on a direct collision course . . . President Beck is preparing to address the world shortly on this very serious and developing situation.

"President Beck?

"The DRUDGE REPORT has been briefed on the details of a new movie set for release—a movie that features the fresh-man all-news cable channel MSNBC acting out phony reports of a catastrophic asteroid hit with the third rock from the sun! In the Steven Spielberg production DEEP IMPACT, inspired by the 1951 George Pal film WHEN WORLDS COLLIDE, due for release

May 8, the all-news cable channel plays a key role in the story-telling.

"The film calls to mind the ethical nightmares of Summer '97, when CNN acted out news in more than a half dozen films in a twisted attempt to product-place the channel: CNN reported dinosaurs being returned to an island; the crash of Air Force One, with the president supposedly aboard; the discovery of intelligent life in a remote galaxy.

" 'The plethora of blatant MSNBC logos & plugs throughout the film bordered on hysterical,' " notes a test screener who attended a showing last week at the PARAMOUNT lot in Hollywood. " 'If I were to guess, I would say that there were more than 30 logos & plugs throughout the 2 hr. film.'

"A change in NBC policy?

"Last year, an NBC SpokesPerson took the high road during the CNN movie mess. When asked if NBC would loan talent and network resources for cinematic exploitation, SpokesPerson Julia Moffett told a reporter: 'We don't feel it's wise to create a blurring of the lines.'

"Nevertheless, the movie casts actress Tea Leoni as a reporter for MSNBC who first uncovers what she believes to be a White House scandal—later learning it's really a super-secret White House plan to stop the asteroid's collision! Breaking news moments, compliments of INDUSTRIAL LIGHT AND MAGIC.

"At one point New York City is completely destroyed.

"Going to be a long night, Brian Williams.

"XXXXX"

Siren off.

March 11, 1998
4:35 am ET

Hate e-mail and flames continue to arrive by the thousands.

"I'm never trusting you again . . ."

"That was really stupid Drudge . . ."

"My youngest daughter's sitting here crying . . ."

"You idiot . . ."

"You should be sued for this!"

Uh-oh.

How many cosmopolitans?

How am I going to cope with Francis X. Clines, New York Times, in just a few hours for my imminent A-Section Above-the-Fold?

I miss Cat.

"That was quite a story on *MSNBC's asteroid* last night, Drudge," says FrancisX, glaring through specs.

"I wanted to provide you with entertaining fodder, Frank," I reply.

Hamburger served—11:48 am ET.

"Do you always pull tricks on your readers?"

"It wasn't a prank, Frank, I was making a point about the blurring line between ShowBiz and NewsReportage . . ."

"Sounds like journalism to me."

"Precisely." Well said. Couldn't have put it better myself.

We don our caps—his fisherman, mine fedora—jump into a cab and head to the DC Fed Courthouse, where the Lewinsky grand jury's in session, and coincidentally, where the judge in Blumenthal versus Drudge has summoned us to his status nudge.

When we arrive, a restive Lewinsky press pack, hungry for scandal scraps, surrounds me desperately.

"Reporters laughed unsympathetically when a squirrel darted into Mr. Drudge's photo-op as he firmly defended his professionalism and insisted he was one of them," Clines writes.

Section A; Page 25; Column 1; National Desk

9:51 pm ET

"ASTEROID MAY BE HEADED FOR EARTH," Brian Williams announces on MSNBC.

The **real** Brian Williams*[#18].

Not the cosmopolitan-induced DRUDGE REPORT Brian Williams. Not the DREAMWORKS Brian Williams.

But the actual tanning-bedded/blue-eyedropped Robo-Anchor!

A real comer, now that Peter appears to have taken old pills,

Tom slurs even the consonants, Dan rarely gets out of makeup and there's so much Vaseline on Barbara's lenses and so much Cheesecloth on Oprah's, they're going to fade into the vanishing point any day . . .

"Tomorrow's NEW YORK TIMES will report on Page One, Column One, Above The Fold that an asteroid is heading awfully close to planet earth," Williams announces with appropriate punch.

"Scientists are concerned that the asteroid, more than a mile in diameter, could hit Earth. Stay tuned to MSNBC for more details as this story develops."

Hey, stop the dish! I was only kidding! About a movie!

Love e-mail and gifts arrive by the thousands.
"I'm never doubting you again . . ."
"Do you have ESP, or something, Drudge . . ."
"My youngest daughter hasn't stopped laughing . . ."
"You're a genius . . ."
"You should win a Pulitzer for this!"
Is this life imitating what passes for art these days?
Did MSNBC hack the DRUDGE REPORT on DEEP IMPACT?
Is last night's performance art tomorrow's real news?
Or do I have a gift I'm not aware of?
Am I prophetic? Psychic? Or just plain prescient?
I race to my newsroom in my upgraded suite.
AT&TWorldNet connection established.
FujitsuLifebook© booted.
Grab the New York Times off the backwires.

It's there!

Section A; Page 1; Column 1; National Desk
Length: 1117 Words.
Graphic: Diagram: "DANGER POINT" shows where the orbits of the Earth and the asteroid (shown in their positions on Feb 13, 1998) cross. Both bodies will be in this area in October of 2028. (Source: Harvard-Smithsonian Center for Astrophysics.)
Headline:
Asteroid Is Expected to Make a Pass Close to Earth in 2028

Byline: Malcolm W. Browne

"The impact of an asteroid one mile in diameter would have devastating global effect, including tidal waves, continent-size fires and an eruption of dust that could cause global cooling and long-term disruption of agriculture."

March 12, 1998
12:08 am ET

The phone interrupts a really good laugh.

FrancisX: "Boy, you're good, Drudge. How did you know?"*[#19]

I mix myself a cosmopolitan.

Yeah, I'm damn good.

For about two weeks.

When the Times is forced to debunk and retract what proves to be a fraudulent deep-impact story. They blame the World Wide Web for inaccurate junk science: "This is what happened. On March 10, a noted astronomer's preliminary calculations on a mile-wide asteroid, called 1997XF11, were grabbed off the internet by reporters . . . alerted by a breathless announcement from the Harvard-Smithsonian Center for Astrophysics."

Section 14; Page 1; Column 1; New Jersey Weekly Desk

March 22, 1998, Sunday, Late Edition—Final

Headline: We're Doomed! Story at 11, Facts Tomorrow

DEEP IMPACT opens May 8 to bad reviews and record box-office. To date it has grossed more than $300 mil worldwide.

"... the shallow babble of the masses."
—Jay T. Harris
Chairman and Publisher of the San Jose Mercury News
University of Nevada, March 30, 2000

In the same way Gutenberg's Bible hastened The End of TheChurch's stranglehold on fifteenth-century Europe, in the same way Thomas Paine rallied troops to fight King George, in the same way Upton Sinclair cleaned up the meatpackers with a single stroke, the internet is liberating the great unwashed.

"Just as public libraries gave everyone books in the 19th century, so the internet should be open to everyone in the next century. Who needs boring tame old newspapers when you can get the Drudge Report, and much else besides, online?" UK Prime Minister Tony Blair's right-hand man, Pete Mandelson, queried the European Media Forum sharply.*[#20]

Sitting in chairs. Signing on in overwhelming shares.

Double. Triple. Quadruple. Every six months.

One website somewhere in the 20th century morphed into 500,000,000 somewhere in the 21st.

With millions and millions and millions of mouse miles to go before freedom of participation has truly been realized . . .

Not bad for a species that once believed the Earth was flat.

The highly respected Agence France-Presse, the oldest newswire in the world, marks the night the gates blew open with a fin de millennium flash:

Dix Dates Dans les Medias en ce Siecle

1901: Guglielmo Marconi sends the first radio waves across the Atlantic, paving the way for worldwide broadcasting.

1920: First commercial broadcast program airs.

1926: John Logie Baird invents television.

1936: The BBC kicks off high-definition public television in Britain.

1951: Edward R. Murrow "See It Now" series launches nationwide television programming in the United States.

1968: A U.S. Defense Department project to link computers lays the foundation for the internet.

1980: Ted Turner launches CNN, world's first all-news network.

1981: The all-music channel MTV goes on the air.

1992: The browser Mosaic brings the internet to non-technical computer-users.

1998: Matt Drudge airs Monicagate on the internet.

Mais alors.

Le Marquis de Modem.

Oui!

Stateside, in one of those serendipitous moments, both the Columbia Journalism Review and Liz Smith declare a line of succession from Marconi to Morrow to Drudge:

Impossible! Fou! Completement errone!

The French have embraced me and my mission from the beginning, but then, they also love Jerry Lewis. After a 1998 appearance at the National Press Club, it's a TFOne camera crew on my tail all the way down F Street.

American reporters consider me beneath them.

They show up in great numbers for my speech, only to write derisively about me.

"No Drudge of a journalist," the Ancien Regime's aqua-clad helmet-coiffed Mary McGrory titles her column.*[#21]

"The online scandal-monger doesn't always have time to check his facts," she scolds.

Moi?

You are the one who told *your* readers "TODAY viewers were shocked awake by Matt Drudge, the online sludge-peddler, alleging Lewinsky's possession of an item of underwear with presidential semen on it. How long will the country endure such noxious fumes and put up with trying to explain Drudge sludge to their six-year-olds over cereal."

Que direz-vous de vos faits, ma Marie?

I accurately reported a dress.

Not inaccurately reported underwear.

Just ask La Judd, credit-grabber.

In your ronde, do you really imagine you have any idea what 6-year-olds already know or don't know, never mind what they're eating for breakfast?

In the same way radio superseded movies, and television superseded them both, in the same way telegraph and telephone superseded town criers and extra-extra boys, in the same way the Concorde replaced the plane and the bullet train replaced the Orient Express and the Lexus superseded the horse and buggy, so too the internet supersedes every mode of communication ever invented.

Except a simple handshake and hello on the street.*[#22]

Not everybody is into superseding.

Avec notre Marie—many, in fact—are *beaucoup effrayé*.

Addressing a media gathering in Reno, Chairman and Publisher of the San Jose Mercury News, Jay Harris, the man who brought the world an erroneous story of the CIA and cocaine in LA, admonished that in an era "where everyone can be a publisher" consumers will be forced to make difficult choices to distinguish credible news from "plain old crackpots."

Crackpots not crack.

Harris also warned that serious journalistic commentary is being replaced by "the shallow babble of the masses."

Ah, the masses, those asses.

"Sometimes I think Matt Drudge and Don Imus have more influence than Bill Moyers and David Broder. And that's a pretty sad thing to say."

That's sad. Too bad.

Hillary Rodham Clinton spoke most eloquently on the matter, February 11, 1998, in the Map Room. It was a Wednesday.

"When you move to the railroad, or you move to the cotton gin, or you move to the automobile, or the airplane, and now certainly as you move to the computer and increasing accessibilty and instantaneous information on the computer, we are all going to have to rethink how we deal with this," FLOTUS admonished.

Millennium Project Dialogue not Grand Jury Testimony.

"As exciting as these new developments are," she continued, "there are a number of serious issues without any kind of editing function or gatekeeping.

"It is just beyond imagination what can be disseminated . . . I don't have any clue about what we're going to do legally, regulatorily.

"Any time an individual or an invention leaps so far ahead . . . you've got a problem."

Would she have said the same thing about Ben Franklin or

Thomas Edison? Henry Ford or Albert Einstein, TimeMagazine's-PersonoftheCentury™?

They all leapt so far ahead they shook the balance.

I say faster. Not slower. Create.

Let the mind wander, daydream, let imagination rule.

Creeks turn into rivers turn into oceans . . .

If technology has finally caught up with individual freedom, why would anyone who loves liberty want to "rethink" that?

"I do think we always have to keep competing interests in balance. I'm a big pro-balance person," Bill's Hill continued. "We've got to see whether our existing laws protect people's right of privacy . . . what do you do when you can press a button and you can't take it back . . . I just wish everybody would take a deep breath . . . I think some of the developments of the last week or two should certainly give anybody pause about what is really going on here."

FLOTUS doesn't have a clue.

For the record, her remarks were cyber-spatially conveyed three weeks after the same wonder wires shot Hill's Bill's ills around the world.

Years later the First Lady warmly embraces the net, launching her campaign for U.S. Senate. In her announcement speech, Clinton promises, if she's elected, all the state's classrooms will be "connected to the internet." Controversy swirls around a musical selection played just moments before she takes to the stage. While backstage practicing her speech, Billy Joel's "Captain Jack"—featuring the lyric: "Your sister's gone out, she's on a date/And you just sit at home and masturbate—" fills the gymnasium at the State University of New York at Purchase and bounces the C-SPAN satellite dish in real time. Rodham and Gomorrah. New York City Mayor Rudy Giuliani jumps on the unfolding PR fiasco, first detailed on the First Lady's first and favorite website. "Any campaign that directs reporters to the DRUDGE REPORT is a campaign without positive ideas," Hillary's spokesman Howard Wolfson chides. "Hillary Clinton is in Buffalo today talking about bringing jobs upstate while Rudy Giuliani is down in the gutter with Matt Drudge."

*   *   *

Another Old Gray Lady, the New York Times' Frank F also been dealing with a bad case of digital indigestion.

Declaring this boulevard reporter's death in his 12/4/ page-above-the-fold-million-circulation Saturday column ...on opined: "Drudge no longer has the power to terrorize the nation's news cycles . . . There are plenty of Drudge wanna-bes on the internet, gassing on many subjects. People turn to the Big Boys not amateur citizen-reporters for news."

More than 1,500 letters are posted on The New York Times' website in response to Rich.

The Old Gray Lady doesn't publish even one.

On the very day Rich's column appears, however, there are more than 600 visits to drudgereport.com from nytimes.com employees.*[#24]

The man who could once close down Broadway with a single stroke can't make a dent on a small little website, not even in his own backyard.

Even with circulation 1,000,000.

A million isn't a billion and a billion isn't what it used to be.

Like FLOTUS Rodham and Old Gray Lady Rich*[#25], even the rabbis start to bitch.

Israel's leading Orthodox Rabbis issue a ruling banning the net from Jewish homes, declaring it "a thousand times more dangerous than television," threatening the survival of the country.

The Council of Torah Sages orders a halt to the infiltration of "sin and abomination" from the internet into homes of the ultra-orthodox.

The net "puts the future generations of Israel in grave danger in a way that no other threat has since Israel became a nation."

The newspaper Haaretz of Degel Hatorah, one of Israel's strictest religious parties, headlines: THE WORLD'S LEADING CAUSE OF TEMPTATION, THE INTERNET.

A "deadly poison which burns souls."

Question:
If Moses were around today would he prefer Apple or PC?
Would he be a Netscape or Internet Explorer?

Would he part the sea with a Palm Pilot?
Deliver the commandments in an AOLChatroom?

<I am your lord>
Lord1: You shall have no other gods but me ☺.
Lord1: You shall not take the name of your lord in vain.
<lightning strike>
Lord1: You shall remember and keep the Sabbath day holy.
Lord1: Honor your father and mother.
Dude666: hey idiot, can't you reed? the topic's britney spears
Reznertrent: dude flame him flame him with nine-inch nails
Dude666: yeah let's flame the poser
Lord1: You shall not kill.
Lord1: You shall not commit adultery.
Britneysp: yeah baby, one more time
Tina13ca: britney, I'm going to a really important party in a few hours and my mom has the perfect top, but she says I'm way to young to wear it. She's just gone out for a walmart run, should I take it anyway?
Lord1: You shall not steal.
JoeBoner: code too high dudes crime in progress tina13ca is going to get her apples polished tonight
Lord1: You shall not bear false witness against your neighbor.
Reznortrent: head like a hole black as your soul I'd rather die than give you control
Lord1: You shall not covet your neighbor's goods, you shall not covet your neighbor's house, you shall not covet your neighbor's wife, nor his manservant, nor his maidservant . . .
Reznortrent: bow down before the one you serve you're gonna to get what you deserve bow down before the one you serve you're gonna get what you deserve
Lord1: . . . nor his BULL . . .
Britneysp: and I want to remind you my upcoming duet with the backstreet boys debuts on trl next week
Lord1: . . . NOR HIS DONKEY!
JoeBoner: lol
Reznortrent: bow down before the one you serve
Lord1: . . . nor anything that is your neighbor's.
Reznortrent: your gonna get what you deserve

Britneysp: and my new cd is in stores now
<Lord1 kicked and banned by op AOL187>
Eminem: HEY. I'M THE REAL SLIM SHADY.
Dude666: cool
JoeBoner: Word.
Dude666: word

AL GORE, JR.

In the beginning there was the word. And the word was: Gore. And Gore said, "Let me be lite."

XXX DRUDGE REPORT XXX
DEC. 7, 1997 XXX

439,500 LBS OF FUEL BURNED BY GORE TO ATTEND WARMING SUMMIT

"The most vulnerable part of the Earth's environment is the very thin layer of air clinging near to the surface of the planet, that we are now so carelessly filling with gaseous wastes that we are actually altering the relationship between the Earth and the Sun—by trapping more solar radiation under this growing blanket of pollution that envelops the entire world," Vice President Gore told the U.N. Global Warming conference of 159 nations this morning in Kyoto, Japan.

In what was one of the most dramatic speeches in recent memory, Gore announced to world leaders: "Whether we recognize it or not, we are now engaged in an epic battle to right the balance of our Earth, and the tide of this battle will turn when the majority of people in the world become sufficiently aroused by a shared sense of urgent danger to join in an all-out effort."

Applause filled the halls of the Kyoto International Conference Center. "We must achieve a safe overall concentration level for greenhouse gases in the Earth's atmosphere."

carbondioxidemethanenitrousoxidehydrofluorocarbonspr-fluorocarbonssulfurhexa chloride. The message is serious. So serious in fact, the DRUDGE REPORT has calculated that Vice President Al Gore is burning more than 439,500 pounds of fuel, or 65,600 gallons, at a cost of more than $131,000 on his 16,000-mile daytrip—just to deliver the warning!

Now that's commitment.

Air Force II's Global Warming Express features an itinerary that takes the vice president from Washington to Florida to Washington to Alaska to Japan and back—all in just 72 hours.

Saturday, December 6, 1997

9:45 a.m.: Air Force II departs Andrews AFB en route Fort Myers, Fla.

12:05 p.m.: Air Force II arrives Southwest Florida Regional Airport. Gate 69-A.

2 p.m.: Vice President Gore addresses the 50th Anniversary/ Rededication, Everglades Municipal Airport, Everglades National Park.

6:40 p.m.: Air Force II departs Florida en route Andrews AFB.

8:35 p.m.: Air Force II arrives at Andrews Air Force Base.

9:45 p.m.: Air Force II departs Andrews Air Force Base en route Elmendorf Air Force Base.

Sunday, Dec. 7, 1:15 a.m.: Air Force II arrives Elmendorf Air Force Base, Anchorage, Alaska.

2:45 a.m.: Air Force II departs Elmendorf Air Force Base en route Osaka, Japan.

Monday, Dec. 8, 5 a.m.: Air Force II arrives Osaka International Airport, Osaka, Japan.

11:15 p.m.: Air Force II departs Osaka, Japan, en route Elmendorf Air Force Base.

12:35 p.m.: Air Force II arrives Elmendorf Air Force Base, Anchorage, Alaska.

2:05 p.m.: Air Force II departs Elmendorf Air Force Base en route Andrews Air Force Base.

Tuesday, Dec. 9, 12:45 a.m.: Air Force II arrives Andrews Air Force Base.

"The extra heat which cannot escape is beginning to change the global patterns of climate to which we are accustomed. Our fundamental challenge now is to find out whether and how we can change the behaviors that are causing the problem."

Gore's plane, a Boeing 707 gas guzzler, burns on average 4.1 gallons a mile.

The complete Washington to Florida to Washington to Alaska to Japan and return to Washington trip calculated from commercial air mileage tables is just over 16,000 miles total.

Gas gallons needed for AIR FORCE II to go 16,000 miles: 65,600.

Applying the average price of $2.01 per gallon of Jet A to the 16,000 mile r/t—the fuel cost alone passes $131,000.00.

There are 6.7 pounds per gallon of jet fuel.

Total pounds of fuel burned on Gore's Global Warming Express: 439,500.*[#26]

XXX

In the beginning there was the word. And the word was: Gore. And Gore said, "Let me be white."

XXX DRUDGE REPORT REVISITS
MID-TWENTIETH CENTURY XXX

NANNY SAYS: I WAS LEFT IN CAR WHILE GORES ATE AT 'WHITES ONLY' RESTAURANT!

"Our parents said to work for good white folks—and that's what we did."

Those are the shocking words of Mattie Lucy Payne, housekeeper and nanny to Senator Al Gore, Sr., and his wife, Pauline.

For more than 30 years, Payne cleaned house and cooked for the Gores on their 250-acre farm in Carthage. It was on this farm where Payne helped raise Al Gore, Jr.

During this period, Payne fought to overcome firmly established social boundaries in the South.

On some occasions in the mid-twentieth century, the Gores would take Payne on trips to Washington, where Al Sr. was Senator.

On those rides, Payne recalls being left in the backseat of the car—as the Gore family dined in 'Whites Only' restaurants.

"Albert Jr. would bring out a sandwich to the car because I was not allowed in the restaurant," Mattie Lucy Payne told a local reporter for the CURRENT LINES of Upper Cumberland.

"We didn't know any better, that's the way we grew up."

Mattie was very close to the Gores. And Al Jr.'s mother, Pauline, expressed her appreciation: "Mattie Lucy is a very special person . . . She always knew the kind of meals everyone liked . . . We think of Mattie as 'one of the family.' "

Pauline Gore even featured Mattie Lucy's recipe for "Farmer in the Dell Chicken" in her published cookbook.

Payne recalls: "When Al Jr. was in college he would come home for the weekend and bring friends. He would say, 'Mattie, fix several different dishes, some greens from the garden.' "

Throughout the years, many of Payne's relatives worked on the Gore farm: "I remember Mrs. Gore saying, 'If they are kin to Mattie Lucy they can come to work," Payne recounts.

And Payne watched as the Gore family groomed Al Jr. for high office.

"Mr. Albert had it in his mind that Al would be in the White House."

But Payne's role in the Gore family history has been diminished in recent years.

Network producers and print editors have opted not to explore Mattie Lucy Payne.

"Segregation in the South is one of those chapters from long ago and far away that is just not spoken about," said a family friend.

"The Gores love Mattie Payne and 'whites only' is a thing of the past. Mattie knows in her heart that the vice president has helped make it that way."

XXX

In the beginning there was the word. And the word was: Gore. And Gore said, "Let me be trite."

XXX DRUDGE REPORT XXX
FEB 13, 2000 XXX

DICAPRIO: GORE FOR PRESIDENT

Superstar Leo DiCaprio tonight stunned the political world when he announced that he is supporting Al Gore for president!

DiCaprio tells TIME magazine in an issue set to hit racks Monday that he is a strong Al Gore supporter—and he is on the verge of joining his campaign.

DiCaprio was even going to take the stage during the New Hampshire primary to cheer his man.

"I was going to just stand onstage and look hard core," the star of The Beach and chairman of Earth Day 2000 tells the mag.

Among the main issues motivating DiCaprio to go Gore 2000—THE EARTH.

"I shouldn't be eating hamburgers, because the methane gas cows release is the No. 1 contributor to the destruction of the ozone layer; and the No. 1 reason they destroy the rain-forest is to make grazing ground for cattle. So it's very ironic that I eat beef, being the environmentalist that I am. But then again, if I ordered the tuna sandwich, I would be promoting the fact that they have large tuna nets that capture innocent little dolphins . . ."

DiCaprio's film, The Beach—which finished in a humiliating second place to Scream 3—has been met by strong criticism over the damage that its filming did to one of Thailand's most pristine beaches.

According to the Associated Press:

"After obtaining permits from the Forestry Department and paying a $110,000 damage deposit, the filmmakers brought in bulldozers to widen and flatten the beach and strip away native grasses, scrub and other vegetation . . ."

Seizing on the film's high profile, activists who had for years unsuccessfully campaigned against the environmental damage to Thailand's parks joined with local residents in a series of demonstrations.

GORE/DICAPRIO 2000

XXX

GEORGE W. BUSH

PRINT IS DEAD

MOVIES ARE DEAD

TV IS DEAD

"Even when I started in 1970, I knew that television was having a negative effect on our society."
                    —Ted Turner—1:00 pm—06/05/96
                    Cambridge, Massachusetts

". . . A lot of us used to be big fish in a small pond, now we are all minnows."
                    —Rupert Murdoch—5:00 pm—02/10/00
                    1211 Avenue of the Americas, New York

"This is really boring."
                    —Katie Couric—12:20 am—01/01/00
                    Times Square, NBC

ODE OF A FAUX ANCHOR

Her first boyfriend was Daddy, I hear tell.
On the ones, she did traffic and weather together.
O&O'd by Mel, she was working in hell.
Somewhere somehow, she wanted To Be
She had to find some way to get
On teevee.
I'm outta here, she cried.
Chopped her skirt. Fixed her face.
Said her mantra. Applied.
I'm joining the race!
She went to breakfast lunch dinner and drink
Glasses of white wine and martinis, served pink.
Radio, cable, broadcast center, in a wink
She became an Andys' twink, I think.
Heyward or Lack?
Don'taskDon'ttellDon'tpursueDon'tblink.

At the center of action.
In everyone's face.
She worked all the buildings
All over the place.
Made love to the camera at 400 North Cap,
Color-coded hair, eyes 'n' shirt to match the map.
With the Capitol as backdrop she did all the gets.
Politicians and movie stars.
And of course, all their pets.
Elevatored to C-SPAN, NBC, guested on FOX.
No longer obscure in a life of hard knocks.
She daytripped cross-country to star in her soap
With the travel and stress, she began using dope.
Officed at 30 Rock, heart full of hope.

I'm your new anchor, she said, high on blow.
Truth's just an out-clause in your contract, my dear.
We're cancelling your show. We're letting you go.
You'll be better off somewhere other than here.
Desperate and lost and feeling unreal
She did what came naturally, she started to steal.
Addicted to airtime addicted to smack addicted to lifestyle.
No way she'd go back!
She cut off her mini, cut it way up to here.
Eye tuck and lipo, a strong acid peel
Augmented her breasts.
Who cares if they're real.

What if they don't notice, our faux anchor feared.
Here they come! Here they come!
The hungry crowd cheered.

So on to the EMMYs, with midriff laid bare
Cover the Carpet and baubles; critique all the hair
A long way from UConn—in fact, *anywhere*—
But as Brian Lamb taught her:
Who Said Life Was Fair.

She went on a diet, she got awfully thin
She threw a big party but the list wasn't IN
No celery for me, I'm losing some weight
But her new boss Bell Blue thought it too late
Security phone call: Have an ambulance wait
No, not on the side but at the Main Gate.
They locked her in Thalians, in a padded gray cell.
No one O&O's me, don't you know I am well?
She screamed, she ranted, she sounded the bell.
12-steps and support groups: You must share, Mirabel.
Adios, my amigos; adieu and farewell
Just hand me the Zoloft. Goodbye! It's been swell.

So playing it cool, she sneaked o'er the fence
Over on Prospect, over and thence
To the set of GH where they tape every day.
Quartermaine, here, and I'm told that you pay.

For services rendered and services due
Services I'll gladly perform on you!

She was picked up at Ralph's on Sunset, it's true
Waving Talk Magazine, she screamed: I'm gonna sue!

It should've been me, I was told that I won.
Years ago, you remember, anchoring NY One?
On the street people whispered, she's over she's done.

So she gave up the parties
She gave up the booze
She gave up the minis
Even gave up The News.
She learned it's a fraud, realized it's all phony
Cashed in her chips and purchased a pony
Off to Montana! Where she could be Queen
Sat at a computer and smiled at the screen
Typing oodles of fluff
For Slate magazine.

DAN RATHER, GET OUT OF MAKEUP!
YOU'RE NEEDED ON THE SET!

NEW YORK—CBS NEWS experienced total embarrassment Friday afternoon when anchor Dan Rather, in full pancake make-up, and Pentagon correspondent David Martin were caught rehearsing coverage of a U.S. bombing run on Iraq—a rehearsal that was mistakenly beamed to television affiliates via satellite!

For twenty minutes, Rather could be seen going through the motions of a bombing.

According to one viewer who witnessed the spectacle, Rather at one point described how it was "not known how many casualties" were caused by the bombings.

The episode turned into a February Sweeps event from hell.

"It felt like WAG THE DOG," a senior news producer at a major-market affiliate tells the DRUDGE REPORT. "I bet the network is living in fear that someone on the receiving end of the transmission had tape rolling."

"This was very embarrassing," one CBS staffer said late Friday. "If I'd seen the report, I'd have thought we were at war."

"It looked like a real broadcast of what was going on," Bill McClure, master control operator at WTAP-TV in Parkersburg, W.Va., an NBC affiliate, told the ASSOCIATED PRESS.

"What is usually a quiet room in the back of our department became very packed," he said.

The network wanted to test new graphics and theme music that would be used to cover the story, according to CBS NEWS spokeswoman Kerri Weitzberg.

Rather did not return repeated phone calls seeking comment. This in from a DRUDGE REPORT reader:

"Drudge, Yesterday afternoon I happened to be scanning my

satellite dish when I came across Dan Rather reporting live on an attack on Baghdad. As I work in the financial business I immediately called numerous colleagues and told them The WAR had started.

"They checked all other networks and they were reporting nothing about this event. I watched for about 15 minutes as they went into very detailed information about the attack. CBS had excellent 3D graphics showing cruise missiles and their routes and targets as well as other various attack methods. CBS also showed LIVE footage of attacks on Baghdad which was quite convincing.

"I telephoned CBS in NY and contacted their International News department. The woman I spoke to was quite surprised at my story. I told her that I was from Canada and she asked me if I was calling from the CBC. I explained that I was watching from my home and she sounded quite surprised. I told her that I had taped the whole event and that I wanted an explanation of what was going on. I gave her my phone number and asked if someone could call me and explain what was going on. After 10 minutes no one had called me so I called back. I asked why no one had called me and she said that high level execs were reviewing the matter. She stated that I was only one of two callers that had called them, the other residing in New Hampshire.

"I gave her my name, address and phone number and suggested someone contact me. I also explained that because I had contacted people in the financial industry a lot of money could be lost reacting to this news, never mind the great embarrassment caused. The details of the report are too long to explain here so I suggest you get a copy of the tape. . . . The tape ended with Rather saying they had to return to what I believe he said was the GRAMMYs and that they would be back with a report later. By the way the broadcast was available on Satellite G4. The so-called attack [was? is?] supposed to happen on FEB 25 . . ."

The CBS development comes just 10 days after NBC's Tom Brokaw was caught on the dish warming up for the evening news—by rehearsing a phony report that Frank Sinatra had died of cancer!

Brokaw said, in a number of takes, that NBC "received latebreaking news that legendary singer Frank Sinatra had died after a battle with cancer."

XXX

"Brokaw, of course, had some of it right. Sinatra did die, eventually. The Most Famous Stranger in the Night died of a heart attack—4 months later in Los Angeles, on an unseasonably cool May evening. That's Time&Again for now. I'm Jane Pauley. We're history."

Since I cover the Makeup out of The Chair, I can report candidly on nefarious activities. I've discovered and revealed dozens of media blow-ups, fake-outs and frauds perped by frauds, fakers and blow-by-blowers.

Getting blown. On blow.

I'm not beholden to them in any way.

I'm not carried on their air.

I'm not a byline in their dirty print.

I don't use their bandwidth.

I have created my own "paper" printed on my own "presses."

Distributed on my own.

Technology has finally caught up with liberated individuals.

On The Strip, we call it "freedom of the brain."

"*What about your Sunday-night coast-to-coast ABC* Radio Show," Cat mocks. "*In a hundred markets, #1 in NYC, LA, and DC in 12+; #1 25–54 AQH, Arbitron, Summer '99. . . ?*"

"That is not the DRUDGE REPORT!" I growl.

Those who think LegacyMedia will survive should rush audition tapes posthaste to CBS CEO Mel Karmazin, Dan's boss (and by the time you read this, probably Tom's and Jane's as well).

Karmazin, the man who singlehandedly destroyed the AM bandwidth, is one of those 20th-century types who moved up from AdSales to become PowerMan. Alas, you can take the PowerMan from AdSales but you can't take the AdSales from PowerMan.

In the early part of '00, the newsroom at CBS's KYW, Channel 3 in Philly, was in an uproar after it was learned that management had sold advertising time to businesses featured in segments aired on the 5 pm newscast.

Staffers, who were ready to walk off the job in reaction to the

blurring of news and advertising, learned of the new policy—
called "sponsored segments"—accidentally, when a photographer was told "I bought this segment" by a business being
featured.

June 29, 2000. 7:35 a.m. ET, New York. WCBS Newsradio 88:
"What happened on Survivor last night?" announcer Jeff
Caplan teases.

Cut to commercial. Traffic. Cut to commercial.

Weather.

Cut to commercial. Top of the NewsClock.

In breaking mode, Mel's boy Caplan leads with the latest
"news" on the parent company's primetime low-budget voyeuris-
tic success, a show taped and wrapped months ago.

Cut to commerical.

A forest fire has blackened thousands of acres in Washington
State . . .

Cut to commercial!

. . . near Hanford, Washington, the oldest and most troubled
nuclear site in America. Seven thousand people have been
evacuated and flames are licking its perimeter, BUT!

Cut!

COMMERCIAL.

There will only be one SURVIVOR! Who Wants to Be a Millionaire.

Commerical. On the ones. Commercial.

NewsClock repeat.

commercialcommercialcommercial. 7:59 a.m. ET.

Addicted to The 000,000 Deal, Karmazin can't let a day
pass without buying or selling someone something everyone
everything.

The price of CBS stock doubled in 1999.

Go back a few more years, it's tripled.

But a million isn't a billion.

"I don't push the envelope. I'm still an easygoing guy who
goes with the flow," Karmazin fibbed to Electronic Media, in an
early '00 feature story titled Wall Street Demigod.

Karmazin, in fact, applies tremendous pressure on his sales
force. But he compensates. "Most people go into sales to make a
lot of money. I want to empower them to do that. As an advertising-

supported medium, it's the only way we're going to make more money."

Demanding nothing less than double-digit increases, Karmazin is reduced to heavy-rotation ads pitching the get rich get erect get off paradigm.*[#27]

"Morale is up. It's no longer about the haves and the have-nots, or the rich guys upstairs with the stock options. There is a difference in the number of shares people have, but everyone owns a piece of the value they create."

Keep those stockholders well.

"He is a moneymaker. He is a super-duper salesman," analysts like to say.

Sell Mel sell.

How much value has Karmazin created?

"Whatever it is, it's not enough!" he told the EM interviewer, in a rare naked-truth moment. "I entered the broadcasting business in 1967, and I don't think of myself as changing things radically." But.

One listen to any of his Owned&Operated "AllNewsAllThe-Time" Top Market Radio Stations turns the listener Mad Ave. toxic. Non-stop advertising. Non-stop.

Content blurs into commercials blurs back again.

10-second liners. 60-second buys.

Metro and Shadow News. Ooohhhh.

Metro and Shadow Sports. Aaahhh.

Metro and Shadow Traffic. Ooh ooh aah aah.

Car fire on The Ten. Ooohhhaahhhohooh. Right there.

That's it that's it!

Mel does not even pretend he's in the *news* business.

Mel is in the business of *business*.

The business of business: the busiest bottom line in The Biz.

Karmazin's "Give us 22 minutes and we'll give you the world*[#28] is more QVC than Tiffany. More Burger King than 21 Club, although I'll wager he wouldn't be caught dead at the former, and he dines regularly at the latter.

Paley's crown jewel of broadcasting, CBS Radio (or is it Premiere? Or is it WestwoodOne? Is it Clear Channel? Infinity? Jacor? Am-FmCapStar?) is a relentless shopper's guide with a whiff of (yesterday's) headlines, (today's) traffic and (tomorrow's) weather—together.

Bette Midler stars in a new sitcom that has critics raving.

Full details next on newsradio 88, WCBS.

On the 1's . . .

"We're #1 . . . we're #1 . . . we have the #1 show in television! And at next year's affiliate meeting, I'll be standing here telling you we've got the top five!"
        —Diana Christiansen, played by Faye Dunaway
        UPS *"Network"* Affiliate Convention, November 15, 1976

THINK #1! VIACOMPARAMOUNTCBS MARRY!

NEW YORK—Tuesday's press conference by CBSINFINITY Karmazin and VIACOMPARAMOUNT Redstone announcing a proposed $35,890,000,000.00 marriage of assets will go down as a modern . . . classic!

Announcing the big one, the feisty Sumner Murray Redstone began: "When you think about the new VIACOM, you really only have to remember a single number. That's number one!"

The #1 cable network group, here and around the globe; the #1 number-one radio group; the #1 number-one outdoor advertising company; the #1 number-one entertainment brands in the most coveted demographic categories; the #1 toilet maker; the #1 TV station group; the #1 number-one broadcast network; the #1 popcorn provider; the #1 number-one television programmer; #1 in rentable home entertainment; the #1 outlet on the planet for connecting advertising with the audiences they need to reach; #1 in number-ones; #1 of all-time in everything numbered; #1 in consumer book publishers; #1 internet; #1 top regional theme park chains . . .

During the Q & A session it became disturbingly clear that many reporters in the room—were actually questioning their own bosses!

At one point, a question was tossed to Melvin Alan Karmazin by a reporter from CBS RADIO, without any disclaimer.

During the press conference, Redstone and Karmazin were asked questions by four reporters with direct ties to the new VIACOMCBS. None dared ask for a raise.

And of course there were a few strays.

When one reporter from TIMEWARNER's CNN stood to ask a question—Redstone, whose father changed the family name from Rothstein, interrupted: "You're from where?"

"CNN," she answered.

Redstone roared: "Do we own you! Do we own you yet?"

The crowd laughed on cue.

Seventh Avenue meets Broadway.

QUESTION: Can you talk about how INFINITY's Internet advertising would match with VIACOM's formal strategy?

KARMAZIN: We believe that branding will be even more important into the year 2000 . . .

REDSTONE: I might just add one point, Mel. We have 300 million worldwide households to drive traffic to all of our sites! . . . When you think about the new VIACOM, you really only have to remember a single number."

#1

wake me when they're done

We interrupt the commercials in The Year of Our Lord DOW JONES $+/-10,000$ and NAS-DAQ $+/-5$K . . .

Yo, Mel! Brand this!

You may o&o WINS, WCBS, KFWB and KNX, but it's The Zeroes.

And the consumer can bypass all of your consuming and see it for what it's worth:

#0

01 October

He may not have been invited to participate in China's giant military parade celebrating the half century anniversary of Communist rule, but VIACOMCBS's Sumner Redstone, sans his betrothed, Mel, told the TIMEWARNER Global Forum gathering in Shanghai that International news organizations should avoid being "unnecessarily offensive" to foreign governments.

As they expand their global reach, media companies must be aware "of the politics and attitudes of the governments where we operate," Redstone warned.

"Journalistic integrity must prevail in the final analysis. But that doesn't mean that journalistic integrity should be exercised in a way that is unnecessarily offensive to the countries in which you operate."

[Drudge daydream: Good Evening, Mike Wallace reporting from Central Beijing. 60 MINUTES has learned that the Communist government here has jailed thousands of political critics and journalists in the past month. But there has never been a finer, more breathtaking show of military might on parade in this capital city. A spectacular event! The mass parade for the 50th anniversary of the People's Republic of China, where hundreds of thousands of flowers decorate the main avenues and squares! Oh, look! Is that our miniature W-88 nuclear warhead passing before the main viewing stand? Hold on. This just in to CBS NEWS. We've just learned that Chinese officials last night *did* go through with the promise to execute hundreds of prisoners. Police insist the prisoners were not dissidents, saying the mass executions are part of a crackdown on crime. The executions were carried out with a single bullet to the head. Now back to the parade, and this beautiful float representing Taiwan.]

Sumner Redstone, chair of the proposed VIACOMCBS (which owns MTVMTV2VH1) took a direct approach toward China's potential.

"There are billions of people in Asia and billions of them are in the MTV generation," Redstone told the conference. "That's what we're after."

The Forum was an extraordinary magnet for the entire global business elite. Dozens of denizens of BillioinaireBarrios*[#29] landed their private jets at the overtaxed Shanghai airport, in the undertaxed zone:

Jack Welch of GENBCCNBCMSNBC; AOL's Steve Case; Jacques Nasser of Ford and Hank Greenberg of AIG. Doug Ivester of Coke and Roger Enrico of PepsiCo; Jerry Yang of Yahoo!, not Yoo-Hoo! Jorma Ollila of Nokia, George Fisher of Kodak, Martin Sorrell of WPP, Robert Kuok of Kerry Holdings. Michael Dell, Ted Turner, Henry Kissinger, Robert Rubin . . .

Gerald M. Levin, chairman of Time Warner, Inc., introduced China's President Jiang Zemin, calling him "my good friend." *[#30]

$$$

May 2000: Levin's underling Ted Turner pulled off quite a coup snagging a private meeting in Moscow with Russian president Vladimir Putin. In the Kremlin's Blue Room, Turner said he requested the meeting in order to catch up with an "old friend." Press reports said Putin and Turner discussed "peace and security issues." As this renewal of old acquaintanceship was taking place, armed investigators rushed the offices of Russia's leading independent media empire. Masked men with automatic weapons, claiming to be tax inspectors, stormed the Media Most Group, whose press titles, television and radio stations have long irritated the Kremlin. Turner's visit with Putin was rotated heavily on CNN. The raid was not.

$$$

Levin presented Jiang with a bust of Abraham Lincoln.

Levin, who did not meet with human rights representatives, told vaunted visitors that Jiang can reel off the Gettysburg Address from memory.

Jiang smiled.

Can Jiang—or Gerry, for that matter—recite Lincoln's letter to William F. Elkins, November 21, 1864?

> "I see in the near future a crisis approaching that un-nerves me and causes me to tremble for the safety of my country . . . corporations have been enthroned and an era of corruption in high places will follow, and the money power of the country will endeavor to prolong its reign by working upon the prejudices of the people until all wealth is aggregated in a few hands and the Republic is destroyed."

Lamenting the obstacles to global American popcultural homo-geneity, Levin said later on CNN, "We just have American cultural imperialism, you know, in this post–Cold War era, there's no countervailing force, that's a significant problem."

Referring to Lincoln's Republic.

Dozens of denizens of BillionaireBarrios boarded their private jets at the overtaxed Shanghai airport, in the undertaxed zone, NextBigThingDeals tucked in their Gucci and Vuitton, Louie brief-cases. Soon to be announced.

[A few weeks later, members of the outlawed Falun Gong spiritual movement walked onto Tiananmen Square in Beijing as a form of silent protest. Dozens were seen being led away by the police to buses. Witnesses said police dragged six middle-aged women protesters out of the square by their hair. "We want bet-ter selection on TIME WARNER cable," one of the members screamed before being taken away.]

The New World Order, Baby.

XXX DRUDGE REPORT XXX
NOV 1999 20:00 UTC XXX

MSNBCNBCNEWSWEEKWASHINGTONPOST MARRY!

NEW YORK—On Wednesday in Mediaville, it was bigger and bigger like a balloon 'til you burst and explode.

In the internet era, when you are a news corporation (and you look like everyone else) you merge and merge and merge and merge and merge until you have the biggest url on the block.

And then you merge again.

The DRUDGE REPORT listened in Wednesday afternoon on a conference call announcing the latest marriage of NBC, MSNBC, the WASHINGTON POST and NEWSWEEK—in a new deal that creates one of the longest acronyms in the history of the medium!

Merrill Brown, editor in chief, MSNBC.com; Leonard Downie, Jr., executive editor, the WASHINGTON POST; Christopher Ma, executive editor, WASHINGTONPOST.NEWSWEEK INTER-ACTIVE; Richard M. Smith, chairman and editor in chief, NEWS-WEEK; Erik Sorenson, vice president and general manager, MSNBC Cable; Marc Teren, chief executive officer and publisher, WASH-INGTONPOST.NEWSWEEK INTERACTIVE; Bill Wheatley, vice president, NBC NEWS, all gathered for a conference call and took questions.

For a moment, the scene turned hysterical as reporters—who might or might not report to those being questioned—tried to navigate through the new proposed media creation.

Felicity Barringer of the NEW YORK TIMES, no longer welcome on MSNBC because of the POST deal, asked the various organs what they planned to do with their "exclusives."

[Ms. Barringer, who has personally not had an exclusive in years, still wants to be prepared to cover them in the event that they occur.]

Will NEWSWEEK break their stories in the WASHINGTON POST?

Will the WASHINGTON POST break their stories on MSNBC?

Will MSNBC break their stories on MSNBC?

"This is a deal between grown-ups," explained Richard Smith, NEWSWEEK.

"We are the biggest website in the world," declared Merrill Brown, MSNBC.

Not just of this world, but of every world. See: Sumner.

During the confusion of the conference call, Leonard Downie, Jr., executive editor, WASHINGTON POST, urged his reporters to leave CNN, which has not yet merged with MSNBCNBCNEWSWEEK-WASHINGTONPOST.COM but has merged with TIMEWARNER-SPORTSILLUSTRATEDPEOPLEMAGAZINE-ENTERTAINMENT-WEEKLYWTBSTNTHEADLINENEWS.COM.

As if the viewer can possibly keep up with any of this.

Who is an MSNBC?

What is a WASHINGTON POST?

Why is a NEWSWEAK?

Merrill Brown, editor in chief, MSNBC.com, used the term "branding" dozens of times during the session.

"Branding" . . . "imprinting" . . . "identity" . . .

The "biggest website in the world" . . .

An immediate controversy erupted during the meeting over whether the NEW YORK TIMES (which previously had an on-air arrangement with MSNBC) was pushed out or did the pushing.

"This deal effectively ends our arrangement with the NEW YORK TIMES," explained Erik Sorenson, vice president and general manager, MSNBC CABLE.

What started as a limitless future between the two orgs— MSNBC even had big plans to build an entire show around the Sunday edition of the TIMES—vanished in the conference room ether.

MSNBC will now use WASHINGTON POST talent for programs like MSNBC NEWS'S NEWS.

"MSNBC.COM, MSNBC CABLE AND NBC NEWS, THE WASHINGTON POST, NEWSWEEK AND WASHINGTONPOST.NEWSWEEK INTERACTIVE ANNOUNCE STRATEGIC ALLIANCE TO INCLUDE NEWSWEEK.COM BECOMING NEWSWEEK.MSNBC-.COM," declared a press release from the companies.

Baby, world order [new].

ABCNEWSNEWYORKTIMES MARRY!

David Westin, president of ABC NEWS, and Arthur Sulzberger, Jr., publisher of the New York Times, kissed and said "I Do" today in a snowy New York.

With this latest greatest urge to merge, it was not immediately clear if either the ABCNEWSWASHINGTONPOST Polling Unit or the CBSNEWSNEWYORKTIMES Polling Unit were headed for divorce or bigamy.

The NYT and ABC will co-produce a daily 15-minute webcast, Monday through Friday, at 1:30 pm ET, simultaneously on both .coms, WestinSulzberger© revealed.

The live webcast will attempt up-to-the-minute political news, and will try to bridge the gap in the cycle between each morning's NYT, GOOD MORNING AMERICA, and each evening's WORLD NEWS TONIGHT and THE VIEW.

The webcast will be governed by the same set of "editorial standards" that exist at the NYT and ABC. Westin&Sulzberger used the term "editorial standards" repeatedly throughout the ceremony.

But Westin may have reason to worry, as Sulzberger has been strongly criticized for sloppy reporting.

Just last month the NYT erroneously reported a longtime photographer was offering up fashion models as egg donors to the highest bidders, a story that was simply an internet hoax.

The NYT had just issued an editorial deriding net journalism as mere entertainment, contrasting the values of the traditional press: "Sound judgment pays homage to speed but reveres accuracy. News judgment can abet courage or invoke caution. News judgment is conscious and conscientious."

In the broadcast arena, ABC and NYT will team to develop and produce segments for 20/20 and GMA.

Editorial control over these pieces will be shared by the two. Westin declared, "We are delighted to be working with the NYT, both for its breadth of reporting and its high 'editorial standards.'"

Sulzberger said, "We are delighted to be working with ABC, both for its breadth of reporting and its high 'editorial standards.' "

Its was not clear at press time if ABCNEWSNEWYORKTIMES would make a play for MSNBCNBCNEWSWEEKWASHINGTON-POST, or if they'll both be sucked into the VIACOMPARAMOUNT-CBS vortex.*[#31]

XXX

Essence of AP Science as reported on Yahoo! Entertainment

BLACK HOLE FOUND NEAR EARTH!

Not to be confused with the black hole at 1600 Pennsylvania Avenue, scientists have discovered a black hole just 1600 light-years from Earth.

Located on a star called V4641 Sgr in the constellation Sagittarius, the black hole alerted astronomers at the Massachusetts Institute of Technology with four bursts of X-ray energy.

"This is one of the fastest we have ever seen," says Bob Hjellming of the National Radio Astronomy Observatory.

AMERICAONLINETIMEWARNERTURNER MARRY!
The Big ONE!

I would've given a billion dollars to see Mel's face.

The man who thought he would be king after he merged with Sumner last year must have been spooked and shaken this morning, logging on from his Trump Tower Penthouse.

Melvin Alan Karmazin has now been topped by a 41-year old geek in khakis named Case who started his career marketing home perms for Procter&Gamble.

And Bill Gates—who outsmarts them all?

He's left with a media empire that consists of something called SLATE and the utterly unwatchable MSNBC.

Mel, meet Bill; Bill, meet Mel.

A hundred billion isn't what it used to be.

Rupert, meet Bob. Ted, forget Jane. Meet Steve.

Everyone: Meet Steve.

New dreamboat stud god to all who play and trade.

It's 2000.

A billion isn't a trillion and a trillion isn't what it used to be.

Are you a zillionaire yet?

Dramatic! Exciting! Levin is a Genius Mind!

Superlatives on the AOLTIMEWARNERCNNFNtickertape throughout Deal Day.

"The Death of Old Media" declares the WALL STREET JOURNAL in a high-IQ op-ed on Tuesday.

"AMERICA ONLINE's acquisition of TIME WARNER marks the beginning of the end of the old mass media, and the end of all serious debate about the triumph of the new," writes Peter Huber.

"For the next decade at least, the new digital bottlers will be in complete control. They will attract the money, define the architectures, and dictate the timetables. The old media vintners will sell out to them, one by one . . .

"Observe that Stephen Case will be chairman of AOL TIME WARNER. The New York Stock Exchange symbol will be AOL. We've lived through superficially similar transitions before, but none as fundamental as this one."

But does D-Day really mark the death of OldMedia?

Isn't it just the latest greatest in a bull market blowout?

When Mel agreed to marry Sumner, not that many months ago, shareholders were told *they* would be #1, led by *the* Chosen Sons.

"Let's make it easy, when you think about the new VIACOM, you really only have to remember a single number: That's number one," Redstone's teeth snapped at reporters.

Sumner, meet Steve. Global, meet Forum. Steve, meet Gerry.

Jiang, meet Honest Abe. Shanghai.

Ted, meet Vlad. Moscow.

Discussions meet Deal meet D-Day!

Big Media is Big Media. Old or new.

With or without a digital makeover.

Fewer and fewer people will run it.

"We are now seeing the dominance of a handful of companies controlling information and how information reaches people," the International Federation of Journalists warns from Brussels. "Unless action is taken to insure journalistic independence we face a dangerous threat . . ."

IFJ Secretary General Aidan White continues in a statement, the deal of deals could undermine "democracy, plurality and quality in media."

"We're going to need to have these corporations redefined as instruments of public service, because they have the resources, they have the reach, they have the skill-base. And maybe there's a new generation coming up that wants to achieve meaning in that context. That may be a more efficient way to deal with society's problems than government," TimeWarner's Jiang Levin has said.

You've got mail. And movies. And music. And magazines.

Can you say Corporate State?

And roller-coaster rides.

And football games. Or hockey. Or women's basketball.

Any sort of gladiatorial contest you might fancy.
And more and more and more.
Fascism, to coin an ancient phrase.
Expiration date, please.
Your social security number, for security reasons.
Orwellism will be lived and loved.
Unless Mel snaps his fingers and commissions a rewrite:
Order. New. World. Make that universe.

With the t's yet to be crossed and the i's yet to be dotted by legions of lawyers given a year to close, and Madonna's Ray of Light warming up the crowd, Case&Levin© announced "the merger of the #1 internet company with the #1 media company."
Zephyr in the sky at night
"New value and new choice."
"Serving consumers."
"New opportunities for entertainment."
"Dream is realized."
"Nothing to do with size."
"Social destiny."
"Change the lexicon."
"The most socially conscious company the world has ever seen."
She's got herself a universe
"A hundred million shares, more or less."
"The merger of the #1 internet company with the #1 media company . . ."

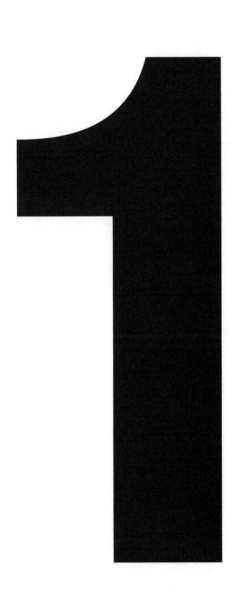

"We're going through a big change ... because of the internet. In a way, it's like saying good-bye to pop culture as we know it."

—Madonna
February 27, 2000
New York Daily News

XXX DRUDGE REPORT XXX
FIRST QTR, 2000 XXX

'MAKING A BETTER WORLD' SWIMSUIT EDITION

The fruits of the proposed merger between AOL and TW are already being tasted.

Starting today, AOL will have exclusive rights to give its 21 million members a sneak peek at the cover of this year's Sports Illustrated Swimsuit Issue!

As an extra merger bikini special, TW's Sports Illustrated will give AOL users an opportunity to get up close and personal with the glamorous models who grace the magazine.

"With the series of model chats available this year, fans of the Sports Illustrated Swimsuit Issue will be able to interact more than ever," Michael Klingensmith, President of Sports Illustrated said in a release.

"We have an unbelievable opportunity to really make a difference, not just in terms of the services people use, but also in terms of the kind of impact we can have on society," AOL HeadCase declared after he announced his marriage to TW.

"This notion of a global interconnection can actually be used for a very good social purpose," agreed TW's Gerry Levin.

"This merger is not just about big business. This is not just about money. This is about making a better world for people because we now have the technology and the instruments to do that."

Last year's Swimsuit Issue covergirl Rebecca Romijn-Stamos offered advice on diet and making the world a better place: "I don't believe in starving yourself, I believe that you should definitely eat when you're hungry. Don't deprive yourself when you're hungry."

Just don't get your keyboards wet.

New World Water. Waterworld, new.

XXX

January 6, 2000
1:01 pm ET
New York

Essence of Entertainment Wire as reported on Yahoo! Finance

HerMajestyQueenElizabethII has conferred the honor of Knighthood on Sir Howard Stringer. In the Diplomatic and Overseas list, Sir Howard Stringer was given the title Knight Bachelor, one of the most ancient and senior ranks of Knighthood. Prime Minister Tony Blair cited Sir for achievements that have left a mark on the 20th [i.e. *last*] century, notably the David Letterman hire for CBS.

As Chairman and CEO of Sony Corporation of America, Howard Stringer has overall responsibility for Sony's Entertainment businesses: Sony Music Entertainment, Inc.; Sony Pictures Entertainment, the parent company of Columbia Pictures and Columbia-Tristar Television; as well as the company's hardware and manufacturing business, Sony Electronics, Inc.; SCA's online game business, Sony Online Entertainment; and the company's location-based businesses.

"You don't have to call me Sir," Sir instructed.

Insiders were surprised at the Queen's grand gesture.

Keith Rupert Murdoch cut a wider swath across the 20th century, and he's been waiting for years to be Sirred.

Rupe has overall responsibility for News Corp.'s Entertainment businesses: Fox Network, 15 TV stations, Fox News, Fox Sports, Fox Family Channel, 20th Century Fox, Fox Animation, Fox Searchlight, New York Post, News of the World, The Sun, The Times of London, BskyB, HarperCollins, Weekly Standard, Australia, and Mushroom Records.

Stateside, insiders wonder who will be medal-of-honored first by the president: Last year's Michael Eisner or last week's Steve Case.

Michael D. Eisner has overall responsibility for Disney Co.'s

Entertainment businesses: ABC TV and ABC Radio, 10 TV and 30 radio stations, ESPN, Disney Channel, A&E, E!, Disney World Disneyland Euro-Disney Asia-Disney, Lifetime, Miramax, Walt Disney Pictures, Touchtone Pictures, Hollywood Pictures, Hyperion, ESPN Magazine, the GO Network, Burbank, Orlando and Walt Disney Records.

Case has supreme responsibility for AOLTimeWarner's Entertainment businesses: The WB Network, HBO, TNT, TBS, CNN, CNNFN, CNNSI, CNN Headline News, CNN Airport, Cartoon Network, CompuServe, Netscape, AOL Moviefone, Digital City, ICQ-InstantMessaging, Cinemax, Warner Bros., New Line Cinema, Hanna-Barbera, Castle Rock, Time, People, Sports Illustrated, Fortune, Entertainment Weekly, InStyle, WarnerBooks, Little-Brown, Warner Bros. Record, Atlantic, Elektra, Sire, Time Warner Cable, Atlanta, Montana, Rhino Records. And Loonytoons.

Remember Ultrasaurus David Geffen?
Maker and breaker of career, lifestyle and presidential choice?
The Cl . . . t in Clinton? The G in DreamWorks SKG?
The Warner Estate. The Lear Jet. The pretty boys.
Tinkertoys.
A billion isn't what it used to be.
Can you even spell Seismosaurus O-v-i-t-z anymore?
Maker and breaker of career, synergy and MOMA acquisitions?
The less-than-ten-percenter who built an empire and left to fail upward. Last seen back on Wilshire, dot.com-ing and dot.going.
And where is Supersaurus Fuchs, the man who created HBO before anyone had cable?
Giganotosaurus Gingrich, the man who engineered a revolution? "I have enormous personal ambition, I want to shift the entire planet. And I'm doing it," Newt proclaimed 1.3.85 to the WashingtonPost's Lois Romano.
Currently shifting the planet, punditing for FoxNews.
Average viewership: 210,000 HHs.
20th Century MediaMonster PowerPlayers replaced by Big-Boys whose egos and portfolios dwarf even theirs.
The latest incarnation of vampires, for the Church of Journalism is hardly holy ground—Murdoch, Malone, Redstone, Turner, Levin and Case, Eisner, Gates, Graham, Salzburg and Zuckerman—all

have sucked the blood from the fourth estate, leaving behind info-tainment formaldehyde.

$$$

Rising from the grave, a new breed.

An online army . . .

. . . who doesn't necessarily choose to march in JiangZemin-Parades.

Sam in his basement in Ohio, Richard from his attic in Seattle, Harry from his Texas trailer, Tokyo Rose trading and tipping off-Street, Marie from her moat in Missouri, Sandy from her SoHo loft . . . "shallow babble of the masses."

Ian from the Republic of the Fiji Islands*[#32], or Eric, for example, live from Wrigley Field. One of 40,000 fans attending a Cubs game who sees the action differently from—possibly better than—the radio announcers and press guys who have space/deadline/editorial limitations. A May Report wannabe, Eric files his flashes during the game on his laptop to his website and e-list.

Gunther from Düsseldorf, Sven from Sveden, Patrini from Moscow . . .

. . . can convey accounts of local events e'ed directly from the scene.

Seen and unseen. Doing it today's way. The *real* Inside.com.

In large cities, where there's noticeable crime—involving gun-fire, perhaps—eyewitnesses can write their own accounts, again, e'ed directly from the scene.

Multiple eyewitnesses can write multiple accounts of the inci-dent as opposed to a single stringer who wasn't there, didn't bother to interview the selfsame witnesses and relies on the po-lice for his story. Citizen reports could eventually find their way into a courtroom as evidence, as with the RodneyKing-BeatingVid.

The ladies and gentlemen of the jury may flip a coin, get it right half the time, but at least with more evidence.

An online army.

Clicking and ftp-ing.

A din of small voices.

Uploading and downloading, if the nation's power grid holds.

Brigades of truth-tellers and mischief-makers, hacking and tracking . . .

. . . as Rupert, John, Sumner, TedGeraldSteve, Michael, Bill, Kate, ArtOchs and Mort watch helplessly from the sidelines, neutered. It's the double-aughts, Guys, keep up if you can.

The world is interesting, I'm interesting.

The DRUDGE REPORT's interesting.

"But you're not a serious reporter, are you?" swipes Cat.*[#33]

A moment for a brief consideration of serious reporting.

June 5, 1998. Flash! In what is being described as a total embarrassment, ABC News erroneously reported the death of Bob Hope in a Special National News Alert, complete with a Bob Hope death-package of clips and performances. ABC reported Bob Hope dead, citing Congress and wires as sources. ABC News broke into regular progamming on the Radio Network with a one-minute special. The report must have been especially humiliating for President David Westin, as Nightline, early in the year, devoted an entire broadcast to the perils of speed-internet reporting and the danger of false information being circulated online without fact-checkers and editors.

July 31, 1998. Flash! In what is being described as a total embarrassment, the Los Angeles Times erroneously reported, quoting one source, the Lewinsky dress had no visible stains. In a front-page scream headline, complete with quotes from legal and government sources. The report must have been especially humiliating for Los Angeles Times' Washington Bureau Chief Jack Nelson, who, early in the year, blasted the perils of speed internet reporting and the danger of false information being circulated online without fact-checkers and editors.*[#34]

"In journalism I think you need to be 100% sure," Nelson pontificated on CNN, facing off.

"I'm a reporter, I'm a reporter," I replied. "I've written thousands of stories and have dozens of scoops. Just because I don't have the clout of a major newspaper doesn't mean I can't get close to truths."

Another thing, Jack.

My news organization never took Staples $$$ for reporting on Staples Center.

Without informing its readers.
Jack.

Print's impotent, Jack.*[#35]
Example: On Friday, April 16, 1999, fading star Sharon Stone is the keynote speaker at the annual meeting of the American Society of Newspaper Editors.

Desperately seeking solutions to their spiraling circulations, The Society has turned to Ms. Stone for insight and guidance.

Sharon dines on two carrots, sips a cup of tea, and snuggles with her husband before addressing the room of nearly three hundred.

Alison Walzer, Editor of the Wilkes-Barre Times Leader, observes: "She makes Jerry Brown seem lucid."

Some Stoned snippets:

"We've done pretty well together, you and I. We've grown. We've laughed sometimes and we've learned some things . . .

"I am fabulous, and you guys are brilliant. I'm taller and younger than before I was famous, and I'm smarter and wittier . . .

"I think both of us try to speak out to the world, you by telling what you've seen.

"Oftentimes, it looks like this kind of slow motion car crash of our humanity. I'm in the car. Not the real car, just the movie car, and you know it's probably not even me, it's probably some stunt guy in a wig . . .

"What are you staring at?" Stone glares, then, fixing the audience with the same cold look she gave Michael Douglas, working on her back in a raw sex scene [Basic Instinct] she continues in a moment of near-coherent clarity:

"I think it's time we sharpen our pencils and in my case, just keep my legs crossed.

"Because we're grown up and we have moved into grown-up places in our jobs.

"It's so important that you take that extra second, slow down, maybe don't be the first to break the story and I, in turn, will try to play better parts and do less stupid movies."

Sharon signs on for BS#2.

Michael, much absorbed in Marriage#2, declines.

£££

Movies? Fade in:
Stanley Kubrick. 1970: A Clockwork Orange, Warner Bros.
Stanley Kubrick. 1980: The Shining, Warner Bros.
Stanley Kubrick. 1999: Eyes Wide Shut, Warner Bros.
Fade out. Case closed. Print's extinct and movies should be.

A moment for a brief consideration of serious reporters.

The J-Man most associated with serious news was Edward R. Murrow, and spare me a lecture about the High Priest of Black Rock. Father Murrow began his serious-reporter career doing serious reporting on puppet shows, Broadway castings and restaurant openings. They don't like to tell you down at the Newseum that E-R-M was first hatched as an entertainment broadcaster.

A perfect Zeroes anchor, if he were handsome enough.

Just ask Peter Jennings, who started his serious-reporter career as a serious-host for a serious-afternoon-danceshow, a gig he probably wouldn't have gotten if his father weren't high up the corporate ladder of the CanadianBroadcastingCorporation.

Executing a perfect pirouette in a romantic network ballet, CBC's Jennings became ABC's Jennings, who became ABC-NEWS's Jennings, who became Roone Arledge's ABCWORLD-NEWSTONIGHT's Jennings.

A perfect Zeroes anchor, if he were still handsome enough.

Just ask Larry King, who launched his serious-reporter career touting racetracks to unsuspecting out-of-towners.

I didn't start by covering puppet shows, hosting a Dick Clark knock-off, or flagging funny fillies in Florida. But.

As Larry himself might say: I know from journalism.

XXX DRUDGE REPORT XXX
SEPT 09, 1999 16:02 UTC XXX

KING FINALLY WINS EMMY

WASHINGTON—If you hang on long enough, if you have enough spunk to put on the suspenders every evening and you don't fall asleep on the air (doesn't matter if your audience snoozes off from time to time), one day, you'll win one.

Larry King, host of CNN's LARRY KING LIVE, received his

first News and Documentary Emmy for Outstanding Interview/ Interviewer at the 20th Annual News/Documentary Awards last night in New York City. It was finally his turn.

King won the award for his 1998 interview with Karla Faye Tucker, which was Tucker's last interview before her execution.

A sampling of King's award winning questions:

"You have been in prison since that day you were arrested?"

"Do they feed you well?"

"When they said you were sentenced to death, who said that, the judge?"

"Because there were axes, a lot of blood. It was a horrible death, right?"

King was an easy choice for Emmy. But it was a bittersweet victory. King was left with the dilemma of celebrating his win knowing that Tucker was executed by lethal injection.

"There will be no dancing on her grave," one CNN producer said.

TIME magazine once wrote of King: "Now, after a half-century of hustling and scratching, after no college and hard knocks, after working as everything from mail-room clerk to racetrack flack, after six marriages, one annulment and five divorces, after being arrested for grand larceny, after declaring bankruptcy, after suffering a heart attack and undergoing bypass surgery, after all this and more, Larry King has finally arrived."

Emmy for Outstanding Life.

XXX

An exclusive Calvin Klein interview was clearly King's best shot at reprising his Emmy win in 2000.

King: "And it's my responsibility to ask, What the heck is the difference in a pair of jeans, really? There's a quality of denim? Will a better jean wear longer? Do I get my money's worth? Can I get too many Calvin Kleins in too many places? Is Calvin Klein everywhere?

"What—frankly, between you and me, what's a better lipstick?"

TV is terminal in ways both trivial and profound:

Tuesday, December 16, 1997
11:50 am ET

Russert breaks into regular programming with a flash.
Based on *two* sources.
"The president has named his dog Luke!" After Russert's son.
Dog's named Buddy. Tim retracts. Evidence.

Wednesday, December 16, 1998
6:30 pm ET

Bernie's probing question to Christiane regarding War.
"Do your teeth shiver when the bombs fall?"
Her answer: "Yes!" with a smile. Evidence.

Friday, June 21, 1998
7:35 pm ET

More dental disarray. Robert Novak on Crossfire.
Live from Betts Theater at George Washington University.
Growling at Lanny Davis, Novak dramatically dislodges his yappers during an unfortunately timed closeup broadcast worldwide.

Tuesday, May 18, 1999
7:15 pm ET

Entertainment Tonight blasts the National Enquirer's exclusive coverage of Johnny Carson's health crisis. "Critics say the report is a blatant violation of privacy," notes outraged newsreader Bob Goen.

The strip runs photos the next day snapped by paparazzi.

Photos rejected by National Enquirer Kingpin Steve Coz on the grounds that they were too invasive. Evidence.

November 30, 1999
2:55 pm PT

I stopped watching TV two years ago, except for an occasional JerrySpringer, even though I did have my very own show during that period; the legal terms of my separation with "Network" insist that I not disparage it. Hereinafter, any and all references to the medium of television are emphatically *not* based on my personal experiences with said network.*[#36] Repeat. Any and all references to the medium of television are emphatically *not* based on my personal experiences with said network.

A hot story is brewing.

I am all over it on the net.

RealAudio pumping.*[#37]

Wires jumping.

Seattle is burning.

Trade reps from 138 countries are attempting to gather in the hope of ratifying agreements re: tarriffs, quotas, exchange rates and buy-backs that have taken years to negotiate.

30,000 protesters are blocking entrances to fancy hotels for their important meetings.

Local cops, caught off guard, have lost control.

Hubris.

WTO interruptus.

The beginning of a new era of civil unrest.

Firebombs, anarchy. Organized on the internet, some say.

Hours into the story, frustrated with my 56k modem connection, I flick on the idiot box to catch some clearer images without the download hassle.

Surf. Surf. Surf. Nothing. Nothing. Nothing.

Oh, I forgot. It's The Zeroes.

Barry Diller's censored Springer, so now even Jerry sucks.

TV is dead.

The people who run on it are sick.

The people who run it all are sicker.

The people who run to watch it are sickest.

One out of three people in America is morbidly obese.

Which is not to say they aren't forever searching for a remedy. On TV.

Diet exercise tarot bankruptcy codependency carb-dependency infos soothe the conscience and motivate the sub.

ColdCutCombo. Load the mayo!

Judging Judge Judy. Couching Dr. Laura. Dreaming of Divorce Court.

Snack-snack-snacking and max-max-maxing credit cards between Rosies and Roseannes while waistlines expand and expand.

Suzanne Somers says two BigMacs without the buns.

Hey, that's no fun!

Hi carbs low carbs no carbs. X-Fat lowfat no fat. Hi-pro lo-pro no-pro.
White sugar white death. Brown sugar Mick Jagger. Body Code.
Sugar busters sugar lusters. Health bar heath bar.
Bar b que. Trail mix. Shrimp cocktail.
Sugarless jello. Bacon cheeseburger.
No fries no shakes no rings.
Small salad. ◄---Waistline
Who tried it? Kenny Rogers.
Atkins Pritikin SomerSizing The Zone.
Who tried it? Larry Hagman. Dean Ornish:
Stay away from fat and eat natural. Who tried it?
Clint Eastwood. WeightWatchers: artificially sweetened yogurt
Roast beef sandwhich nonfat cheese and Duchess of Yorkshire pudding.

Jenny Craig
Carbs 60% of diet
With 4 oz. roasted chicken. Burn
150 cals per orgasm, Lewinskies: 90.
Oprah takes Hellers to top, complains to
Publisher she ain't losing lbs. Aniston does,
On full fat cream cheese porterhouse idaho baked.
Don't eat fat with carbs. Do eat fruit. SnackWell.
Butter-busters: eat more weigh less. Butterfly lamb
Slicked finger egg roll. Get Skinny on Fab Food. Up with
Protein. Insulin. Down with Carbs! Type O's eat red meat <--Waistline
Type A's eat veggies. Who tried it? Elizabeth Hurley.
Fondue Bourguignone bernaise fried chicken
Alcohol for Buzz. Who tried it?
Marlon Brando.
Caesar.
Salad.

"Television has turned people into couch potatoes. . . . The more you watch the less chance you'll get anywhere, the less you're going to accomplish," Robert Edward "Ted" Turner speechified in Cambridge, Massachusetts, Wednesday, June 5, 1996.

Surf. Surf. Surf.

Nothing. Nothing. Nothing.

While CNNUN is in a stock market report, I notice on my PC, which is streaming RealAudio from a local Seattle affil, that a series of explosions has rocked the downtown area.

Police cast a giant cloud of noxious gas over the core of Seattle.

Resaca. Resaca. Resaca.

Nada. Nada. Nada.

I just know if an explosion rocked Pristina, Christiane Amanpour would rush to the airwaves in breaking news urgency, onions under fingernails, breathlessly reporting the sound of an atom splitting.

Jamie would be feeding the script in her ear from State.

Bernie and Judy would slug it exclusive:

[BACK]

————

4/15/99

————

There are reports tonight of complete carnage in the wake of continued NATO bombing in Kosovo.

"On the ground, smoldering skeletons and a woman cut in half . . . a man's head lying in a field with the wind blowing his brown hair against the grass, and corpses lying in a squalid hospital nearby," reports the London Independent.

But there appears to be a silver lining.

At CNN headquarters, things are booming with the bombing.

Press release after press release zap the wires with Crisis-InKosovo numbers. "In primetime the network posted a 1.1 rating ... an increase of 22%," rejoice CNN's David Bittler and Alison Rudnick in a release moving along the APExpress.

"The network series of four primetime Special Reports on the crisis posted a 1.2 rating and delivered 895,000 households."

Bittler and Rudnick point out increase by increase, daypart by daypart.

Late Edition, airing Sunday on CNN, "experiences increases of 100%" during last week's NATO runs. Crossfire jumps 38%. Inside Politics surges 80%.

The practice of issuing vaunting press releases celebrating increased viewership during wartime is not a CNNExclusive.

Earlier this week ABC News played up a win for the 90-minute broadcast "Bad Options: The Crisis in Kosovo," even breaking the numbers down into MadAve-friendly demos.

Koppel's Kosovo Coverage Kicks Conan!

ABC News declares in a release: In adults 25–54, the Crisis in Kosovo pulled 2,210,000 over NBC's 2,150,000.

LettermanKilborn trailed with 1,890,000, ABC reminded . . .

[END] [BACK]

"It's a frightening thing, all this corporate ownership," Ted Turner pontificated not so long ago.

Then he sold out for a hundred million TW A-class global shares.

"After you get to 100 million dollars, it gets real hard to spend it all on yourself," Turner boasted to Brokaw, whom he never could purchase, although he tried pretty hard. Brokaw's mouth was hanging open, slavering over so many zeroes.

A hundred million isn't a billion and a hundred billion isn't a trillion and a trillion isn't what it used to be.

Probably hard to give a hooty, raking in that POKEMON booty.

Turner wouldn't hear the boom boom boom in Seattle, Pristina, or anywhere for that matter.

I pound my remote.

Nichts. Nichts. Nichts.
"Where's Seattle?!#*!"
"Bitch bitch bitch . . ."
The same channels went live last month—for hours—when a shooting went down in the city's marina.
That was on message, I suppose.*[#38]
The Nets prefer local shootings to protests against world systems they own and operate.
Surf. Surf. Surf.
DirecTV© channel #539. Showtime 3. West. Stop.
Ned Beatty preaches Paddy Chayevsky dialogue.
Ned: "There are no nations. There are no peoples. There is no America. There is no democracy."
Finally. WTO coverage.
Ned: "There is only one holistic system of systems. One vast interwoven interactive multivaried multinational dominion of dollars. Petrodollars electrodollars multidollars is the international system of currency which determines the totality of life on this planet. That is the atomic and subatomic and galactic structure of things today."
RealAudio: Police are firing pepper spray into the crowds and protesters have started hundreds of blazes all over downtown Seattle. The mayor has outlawed the use of gasmasks by civilians.
Ned: "The world is a collage of corporations inexorably determined by the immutable bylaws of business. The world is a business. It has been since man crawled out of the slime."

Hold on? What year—?
"1976. Faye Dunaway. Best Actress," Cat snaps. *"MGM. Directed by Sidney Lumet. Chayevsky wanted his credit removed from the final cut . . ."*
I could watch this all day, but drudgereport.com is in BreakingNewsMode and RealAudio reports chaos resulting in massive arrests.
There's got to be something on one of these networks by now.
\zap. Nothing. /zap. Nothing. \zap. Nothing. /zap.
DirecTV channel #356. MSNBC. Stop.
Bob Wright, CEO of NBC and Chairman of the mothership,

announcing the official launch of a public internet company bearing the name NBC Internet, Inc. (NBCi).

Bombs Branding In Mid-Air.

Rien.

/\zap.

Ned: "There is only IBM ITT and ATT. DuPont Dow Union Carbide and Exxon. Those are the nations of the world."

I am starting to understand deeply that Nets don't have the guts to cover globalism riots in real time.

They're yesterday's way.

Safe and mushy and late to everything.

Last-century frauds banding together to flee into the next.

A wave of breaking bottles crashes across the city street, someone cuts a cable, knocks off a satellite, halting the feed to FNC's (dtv#360) Hannity and Colmes.

After the market closes and the channel exhausts all JonBenetLewinsky chat, it stumbles into riot coverage.

MTV NEWS is nowhere to be found during anarchy, even though many of the thugs on street level blasted the heavily rotated Chemical Bros. Out Of Control from cars and boomboxes.

MTV youth aren't programmed to get upset about their corporately conceived destinations.

Isn't MTV really just a VIACOM production—which will soon marry CBS—which will own .33 of everything on cable?

MTV rebellion: a Loveline episode between shotgun-bong hits.

Tom Brokaw–aged Kurt Loder will feign concern as he introduces the new buzz clip, sponsored by PEPSI: "This Rage Against the Machine World Premiere video, brought to you by Nike . . ."

TV is dead.
The people who run on it are sick.
The people who run it all are sicker.
The people who run to watch it are sickest.

But one of my legacy habits is to catch the East Coast feed, compliments of the dish.

I get ABC's Nightline at 8:30 pm PT.

In Seattle, the U S of A, fires still rage.

National Guard.

Curfew.

Gasmasks outlawed.

But I can't believe my eyes.

Nightline is working a bogus border tip, digging for bones that will never be found in Mexican graves.

There is not a scintilla of coverage on the cries issuing from protesting countrymen, who are very much alive.

There's no symphonic soundtrack, no spiffy "Battle in Seattle" graphics to tell the story of tens of thousands of people screaming above the satellites, hoping the world will hear a story the networks refuse to tell without a sneer.

"Not since the days of the Vietnam War and the Civil Rights Movement has the entire downtown core of a major American city been seized by popular uprising; rarely has so diverse an array of groups linked elbows against a common enemy, in this case the faceless forces of globalization," a newspaper reports in fresh editions.

Announcing the afternoon headlines in the old/new spirit of Extra! Extra!, vendor Paula Rozner calls out: "Mad river of people floods the streets!!!"

Pictured below, a protester dressed as a sunflower blocks a limo carrying Secretary of State Albright, for whom the world is not enough.

Her raw lust for control on a geopolitical scale is beyond ego and ambition and a hot new St. John outfit from Neiman's calculated to make her Chinese counterpart overlook the USA's bombing of his embassy in Kosovo.

"Those who graduate today will live global lives," Albright informed Harvard students in a recent commencement address.

Trapped over lattes in the lobby of the Westin Hotel as antiglobalists rage outside, I'll bet Number One at State is reassessing the concept.

Number Two at State—Talbot, Strobe—is a no-show.

"I'll bet within the next 100 years, nationhood as we know it will be obsolete; all states will recognize a single global authority," TalbotStrobe said in a TIMEprobe. "All countries are basically social arrangements . . . no matter how permanent and even sacred they may seem at any one time . . . they are all artifical and temporary."

Number One EOP, his putative boss, agrees.

"We think it's a great challenge to marry our conceptions of social justice and equal opportunity with our commitment to globalization," Bill Clinton declared at a summit in Florence, Italy, a few weeks ago, where his Insignificant Other picked up a "global law" award, "a way that requires *governments to empower people* with tools and conditions necessary for individuals, families, communities and nations."

Sorry, Mr. Clinton. Here, *people empower governments.**[#39]

And by the way, Ted Koppel's hair left the building years ago. Another thing. TV is dead.

My WTO coverage on the internet garners me a place on the Ten Websites That Will Change The World list composed by the world trade organizers and conferred on me the next time they all got together in Davos, Switzerland (much harder to reach to protest in than Seattle).*[#40]

This time they call themselves the World Economic Forum.

I reject the honor the same way I reject Walter Cronkite's comments to the BBC that very weekend: "American people are going to have to yield some sovereignty to an international body to enforce world law," America's most trusted man intones portentously.

To paraphrase Marx (GrouchoNotKarl), I don't wanna belong to any club that would include me.

**January 17, 2000
8:20 pm ET**

CNBCMSNBC—Deep Analysis*[#41]
Eve of New Hampshire primary, 2000.
Host: A very blond Chris Matthews/Hardball—425,000HHs
Actual Transcript:

begin

CM: "Well. Let's go to Claire Shipman. Talk about Al Gore tonight. You know, Gore looks really good. What is going on with him physically. He seems to have more hair than he used to. Is there something going on out there?"

Claire Shipman (whose husband, James Carney, Time Inc., has good hair): "I am so glad you asked me that question, Chris, I really want to talk about Al Gore's hair, because that is a big story. I have no idea. I mean, you know, he looks like he's been working out for the last 6 months, you know. He's trim, but I don't know anything about his hair, but I'm sure he'll be glad to know that you think he looks good, Chris."

CM: "Well, he looked very very buff tonight . . ."

CS (shifting politely/uncomfortably): "Don't drag me into this, Chris. I gotta cover him."

CM (persisting/perspiring): "Well he looked very buff and I noticed the thickening of hair there, which I didn't know where that came from."

CS (pissed): "Chris . . . !"

CM (impervious): "The hair—maybe he's on some Viagra or whatever. Well, anyway, maybe Rogaine."

CS (emphatic): "Don't drag me into this."

CM (dismissive): "Hey, we'll get back to substance next time. Thank you, Claire Shipman . . . you're watching Hardball."

And *FADE* to commercial.

end

Always. Fade.

And laugh. Always. Laugh.

I have some old pictures of ChrisMatthews from *his* campaign years. Dark-haired, buff, out there with Speaker of the House Tip O'Neill. He's got the same colored nose, but how did he get so blond? From a bottle? Maybe he's on Viagra or whatever.

Only his hairdresser knows for sure.

Gotta get her number to confirm.

Chris Matthews's exhange with Claire Shipman is a prophetic sign that Campaign2000 will hardly turn on issues. Matthews, Williams, O'Reilly, Geraldo are determined to cover every step, slip and slut on the trail.

Imitation being the sincerest form of pandering and all.

It's really showbiz, every last frame.

Polished, petty and perfumed.

Strike perfumed.

Behind the scenes, reporters traveling with John McCain are obsessed.

E-mails fly through wire, newsrooms gurgle with giggles.

Obsessed.

Not with his policy. Not with his campaign style.

Not even with how he might change America or destroy the DeathStar.

They are obsessed with the Arizona senator's alleged body odor!

"Don't they sell Ban west of the Mississippi?" an A-ListMedia-Player e's.

"The stinky McCain thing isn't true!" IM's Lucianne Goldberg, NYC book agent who knows all.

Am I out of grade school yet?

More to the point, are the people who decide what airs and what doesn't?

Who appears and who doesn't?

"No. She's black."

"He's got an accent."

"Avoid women over fifty."

Verbatim guidelines to a booking producer of a cable news show who talks to me on condition of anonymity.

"They want youth and good looks," my source says. "I'm always suggesting interesting people to have on, you know, try to break it up a little. But I'm constantly overruled.

"Today, I had one of the worst single days of my life! I booked a guy to be on the show who had an altercation with Joe Lockhart at the White House. He was making news. I had the video. He even made plans to set up an ISDN line at our studio so he could simulcast his appearance on his radio show.

"A few hours before air, the suits pull the plug. 'He's too old,' my boss tells me. The guest is already at the studio but I have to boot him anyway. *Then,* we *use* the video and discuss *him* with *other* guests. I swear, I'm physically ill. I'm so ashamed . . ."

The people who run on TV are sick.

The people who run TV are sicker.

The people who run to watch TV are sickest.

Thick, thicker, thickest?

Chris Matthews left the building fifty pounds ago.

Another thing.
TV *is* dead.

January 1, 2000
00:00 UTC

Around the world it blasts off with hardly a hitch. Minimal computer problems, zero terrorist blowouts. Just mounting excitement rolling from country to country, zone to zone, people to people—purging resentments, Forgiving and Forgetting, as Mother Love would say pre–Robin Givens—as the ball of time unravels.

Cameras and satellites beam and bounce.

Walt was right. It's a small world after all.

For a moment I think, maybe TV still serves a purpose.

Maybe it's valid.

"I can't believe you've got the telly on. You keep telling me it's dead," Cat reminds me, smirking.

"Maybe it's not quite dead. Maybe it's only on life support."

"I can't wait for NBC's coverage in Times Square. Tom Brokaw promised he'd have the best seat in the house. And Sting is performing from SNL's stage 8-H."

Brokaw? The man who bailed last spring from a planned debate between us to be moderated by John Kennedy Jr. at PC Expo?

I forgive thee, T.

Today, there's certainly been a reason to keep the set plugged in. How else could I possibly witness the celebrations of all the nations. I have the illusion I'm there, participating:

In Sydney, Australia, where the crowd is naked and drunk.

Spikey? The man who told the New York Press, "The guy didn't have the fucking Lewinsky story. He didn't know what the story was. To say that he broke the story is bullshit."*[#42]

Let bygones be by—I.

At the pyramids, tripping on lasers and Tangerine Dream.

The Acropolis, sans George Stephanopoulos.

"We've all seen the rise of the increasing power of Larry Flynt and Matt Drudge . . . a whole lowering of standards of . . . acceptable political discourse, which is not a healthy development."

Ah, what the hell, hope you're swell.

On to Paris! With Barbara Walters, I board the ferris.

I forgive our boss, David Westin, memo-writer supreme, who tried to cut me and my national radio show off at the knees.

"What about your performance at KABC, 790 AM in Los Angeles, #2 market for audience, #1 for advertisers," Cat brags. *"Drudge: #1 all formats all demos; #1 25–54 male/female; #1 35–64 with a 12.3 share AQH; average listening time 89 minutes, Arbitron, Fall '99; #1 . . ."*

"Wake me when you're done."

I'm with the Queen at the Thames, igniting the flames.

I inhale oxygen with Billy Joel at the Garden.

2000 finally hits the United States of America and Will Smith performs a spectacularly graceful crotch-grab at Q's Lincoln Memorial Joint. Kenny Rogers mouths The Gambler noncommittally. Elvis, Circa '76.

I forgive Peter Bart, Daily Variety*[#43] Editor, for trashing me publicly while his marketing mavens shower me with payola (caps, sweatshirts and Cannes film festival bibles) to ensure their site's linkage. Besides, green is not my best color.

I forgive NYC's WNBC-TV's VP/News Director and Friend of Hillary's, Paula Walker Madison, for airing a story declaring me "infamous and largely forgotten" on the 11 o'clock news during February sweeps.

On the same day the station's VP of Sales e-mails:

"I am a longtime fan and visitor to drudgereport.com. While I do not consider our site to be drudge-worthy today, I think it will be soon. Would you consider a link to WNBC.com?"*[#44]

I forgive I forgive I forgive. At least for tonight.

Even the city of flesh at eop.gov who refuses to respond to questions posed by the press based on my reports, who's lectured extensively on my site's virtues and lack thereof, but who's got me at the top of his bookmarks. Say it isn't so, Joe.

Lockhart, you'll always be in my heart.

In Times Square, the Waterford crystal ball begins its descent and 3,000,000 disparate souls joined at the hip count it down together. Ten. Nine. Eight. Seven. Six. Five.

I choose to soundtrack with my favorite Disney. The Disney greats. I've studied every one and lived a few.

The Second Star to the Right. Give a Little Whistle.

It's a Small World After All:

"There's so much that we share."

Four. Three. Two.

"It's time we're aware."

A record confetti-drop fills the air.

00 00 00 00.

I hug Cat. Cat hugs back.

I burst into tears.

"This is really boring," Katie Couric pronounces on NBC.

"What a bitch!" Cat says, breaking our embrace. *"Damn, I lost my vibe."*

P.O.W.E.R. O.F.F.

Tee.

Vee.

Is.

Dead.

Yo, Katie!

You may have the best seat in the house for the biggest party in the history of New York City, you may have just re-upped for record morning money, but it's Zero, Honey.

And if you're bored, it's because . . .

you're boring

Who killed television?
A.C. Nielsen, that's who.
What turned it from golden to moldin'?
Ad revenue, that's what.
In the end, content's ruled by nothing more than numbers, broken down by sex/sexual preference, race/racial preference, faith/faith-based preference, economic status, educational status, TRW and IRS status.
Does your baby like BeechNut® or Gerber's®?
A paltry thousand or so viewers, acting as people-meters, gauge what's hot, what's not. What's cold. What's old.
Accordingly, ad dollars ebb and flow.
Not an environment particularly conducive to creativity.
Not an environment for talent, which is viewed with hostility.
Fiscal responsibility? An impossibility!
Books are cooked to fit PR, and nothing's based on true ability.
And forget about some chance civility.

The media PowerPlayers think they're destined to run a world dominated by lucre. We're so apathetic and accustomed to being entertained, we're dangerously close to saying: sure fine whatever lower lower yeah that's it. Hot pursuit on the Ten. Shots fired by a two-year-old.
They're not worthy and their hands are dirty.
They're merely recklessly ruthless, egregiously greedy and shockingly petty. Moreover, they aren't as smart as they think they are and they've developed a nasty habit of imposing their truly mediocre taste: see set for CBS's seventeenth revamped Early Show.
They wish to rule all content. They believe they can amuse/anesthetize/program us with accelerated SafeSpeech Viloporn.
Compressed by digital CASH and dictated by the Stock Market,

The National Lottery. Sold by the Advertising Group and censored by DrugCzar General McCaffrey:

"An on-strategy story line that is the main plot of a half-hour show can be valued at three 30-second ads," the general testified quietly to Congress, referring to discounts on legally required license-mandatory Public Service Interruptions swapped for pre-approved do-gooder scripts. Big Brother is watching.

Thank you, Karmazin. Sell Hell Mel.

Flat. Dull.

Boring.

Uh-oh.

World boring?

If the world turns boring, then I'm boring. You're boring.

And worst of all, the DRUDGE REPORT is boring.

XXX INTERNET AT RISK XXX

"The whole idea is its universality. You should be able to use the web for anything which is information. The power of the hypertext link is the fact that it can link to anything." But. "I didn't envisage a system for electronic commerce," mourns Tim Berners-Lee, inventor of the World Wide Web.

Last century's acquisitive UltraSizmoGigantoSupersauruses—fighting extinction—are grazing. Co-opting our turf.

Monitoring our movements. Profiling our purchase patterns.

Venture-capitalizing all aspects of modern consumerist life.

Even religion, see: iBelieve.com.*[#45]

"We hope and expect to make a profit before the next five years," says Ben Chereskin of Madison Dearborn Partners, majority owner, referring to his slice of a faith industry worth $3 billion.

Listening in on our love lives, using insidious tracking devices:

Media Metrix©, PC Data©, Project Echelon©.

In a return appearance, back to murder another medium:

Nielsen/NetRatings©.

Be afraid, 21st Century Traveler.

Don't let them do to the internet what they did to all the rest.

Essence of PR Newswire as reported on Yahoo! Science

INTERNET UNIVERSE EXPANDS 22.7%

Total User Increase: 59,000,000 to 119,000,000. 47% Female. 53% Male. Females online jumped 32% out-stripping 20% of growth for men. Males still spending more time online than females. Gap growing, reports Nielsen/NetRatings©. Men spent more time online per month than women. Difference increased by 2 hours and 12 minutes. "As the gender gap closes we still continue to see men and women differ in their use of the web," said Allen Weiner, vice president of analytical service for Net-Ratings©. "Men tend to flock to news and information sites that present deep and rich information, while women gravitate toward sites that provide topics related to health and well-being, with an accent on efficient use." Number unique sites visited per month decreased 40%, from 15 to 9; number page views seen per surfing session increased 68%, from 19 to 32. "As people become more familiar with the web, we're finding that people prefer to visit a smaller set of specific sites. They tend to spend more time on few sites, but view more pages, suggesting that the larger sites are becoming broader and deeper," said Weiner. The number of ad impressions delivered by the top advertising domains grew significantly.

¢¢¢

Whether online offline NewLine FineLine, the Corporate State would have you believe that you must begin and end your day praying to its God of Demographic Dollars.

In the agglomerating climate—by default and old addictions—banners, pop-ups and java jumps will be required to conform to MadAveThink. Trapped and suffocated by sheer tackiness: see set for ABC's forty-ninth revamped Good Morning America.*[#46]

Profile-market-research drek risks doing to the net what it did to the tube.

In order to make a living online, most of us have to sell ads.

Frankly, I'm not so sure I'd be able—dare I say allowed—to launch my beloved DRUDGE REPORT and make an impact in today's environment.

I certainly can't afford ad space on the aoltimewarner-pathfindernetscape marquee to herald my arrival. I certainly can't afford a Rolodex launch-party staged under Miss Liberty's torch, which worked *soooo* well for Mrs. Evans' TALK. I certainly can't afford the monthly premiums for a premier publicist.

I can't afford product placement, event tie-ins, billboard buys.

I suppose I could do some performance art, but these days that could involve heavy artillery and I'm a peaceable guy; I don't crave the sort of negative attention showered on the Columbine killers and how else do you make the cover of TIME, NEWS-WEEK, TV GUIDE, INTERVIEW or VOGUE?

Fortunately, I have a good head start in www territory.

Seven years ago, when I launched my website, all I needed was a sense of adventure and a little positive reinforcement, which was often a mantra I provided for myself:

The world's interesting. I'm interesting. You're interesting.

So I'll *never* relinquish my page.
I will never be owned by Sumner.
I will *not* kiss Sir Stinger's ring.
Not duped by Rupe nor rope-a-doped by Killer Diller.
I will not be spiked by KayGraham, ArtOchs, Mzuckerman.
My teeth won't shiver for Bernie Shaw, I won't ask Larry King which is the best lipstick.
I'll never compete on Who Wants to Be a Millionaire, TRL, Survivor. Or McLaughlin's Group.
I refuse to be comped in Vegas, attend a White House Dinner, or live in any property owned by Donald Trump.
Drudge will not be polled. Drudge will not take census.
Drudge will not be keyworded on anyone's IPO.
Drudge will take his Tootsie moment, but with photo approval.
Drudge will outlive Clinton.
I don't do windows, but I *do* do Windows©.
This . . . is the DRUDGE MANIFESTO. A work in progress.
CLICK

Double Click.

DEFRAG

C:\\delete *.*

The authors would like to thank each other.

#A

MISTAKES WERE MADE
DRUDGE National Press Club Q & A
June 2, 1998

MR. HARBRECHT, President: Well, Matt, I wonder if you would define the difference between gossip and news, then, please.

MR. DRUDGE: Well, all truths begin as hearsay, as far as I'm concerned. And some of the best news stories start in gossip. Monica Lewinsky certainly was gossip in the beginning. . . . At what point does it become news? This is the undefinable thing in this current atmosphere, where every reporter will be operating out of their home with websites for free, as I do. I don't charge. It's a question I'm not prepared to answer, because a lot of the legitimate news cycles—the Associated Press, for example, will issue news alerts, a recent one being an anthrax scare in the Nevada desert, where a group was targeting the New York sub-ways. AP news alert. Berserk. It went all the way to Janet Reno commenting. It turns out it wasn't true. I think that was some gossip. [Laughter]

MR. HARBRECHT: Let's talk a little bit about the Monica Lewinsky episode for a moment. I guess one could say you did "out" that story by reporting that Newsweek had reservations about reporting it. The story came out. The American people made a judgment, and Bill Clinton's approval ratings in the polls have gone up 20 points. People consistently tell pollsters they don't want to know this kind of information. They don't want to know this kind of stuff. And they blame the news media and they hate us even more. Would you comment on that?

MR. DRUDGE: Well, I disagree with the question. Ask Geraldo or Chris Matthews if the American people dislike it. Their ratings are doing quite well. I think they just expanded Matthews to two hours. I disagree with that. This is a story that's developing, that's serious. When I broke the story, I had it for four days to myself exclusively where I was reporting details, quite frankly, Newsweek didn't have at that point. So I did some original reporting with that. I barricaded myself in the apartment. I was terrified, because from my Hollywood apartment a story of this magnitude was being born. I remember I teared up when I hit the "Enter" button on that one that night, because I said, "My life won't be the same after this." And it turned out to be right. I think it's—as the front page of all the newspapers say, this thing is yet to be determined. I hope the American people will not let someone who has lied potentially in office stay in office. But that's our call. You know, we've been here before and we've made these decisions before. We're letting the court do it. If you've noticed, the tapes have not been played in public, the portions of the tapes I have heard. And the people who are in possession of these tapes, I believe, are letting the courts take care of it. Some of the tapes are quite graphic in details I have heard that I ensure you will take up several news cycles once aired. So I would—I'm not convinced this thing is DOA or the American people have dismissed it as private life.

MR. HARBRECHT: Do you see your methods and your medium as controversial in and of themselves, or are they contributing to the degradation of serious or hard traditional journalism?

MR. DRUDGE: Well, you know, the editor of Civilization magazine, Adam Goodheart, wrote a great op-ed in the New York Times talking about "Is this really something new, this type of fast reporting, this competitive, very competitive"—I'm part of the headline generation. He maintains it was a going back to our foundations when the press was found in quite a different atmosphere, when the press would report that the president's mother was a common prostitute brought over by the British army. Imagine if someone did that now. We have a great tradition of freedom of the press in this country, unpopular press. If the First Lady is concerned about this internet cycle, what would she have done during the heyday when there was 12, 13 editions of a paper in one day? What would she have done with that news cycle? That's the foundation. That's what makes this club great is the tradition. And I think we have a tradition of provocative press. And I maintain that I'm the new face on that. I'll take that for a season. But a lot of the stuff I do is serious stuff. I was first to report that the encryption was missing from a Loral satellite, for example, a couple of weeks ago. I didn't see the main press reporting that one. So not everything I do is gossip or bedroom. To the contrary, I think that's just an easy label to dismiss me and to dismiss the new medium. But I'm excited about the launch of this internet medium. And again, freedom of the press belongs to anyone who owns one. (Applause.)

MR. HARBRECHT: How much do you embroider or make up in your online items? (Laughter.)

MR. DRUDGE: Now, which person here asked that question? (Laughter.) Well, no one's raising their hands. None. Everything I print from my apartment, everything I publish I believe to be true and accurate. I put my name on every single thing I write. No "Periscope" here. No "Washington Whispers" here. (Laughter.) I put my name it; I'll answer to anything I write. I'll make mistakes. I'll retract them if I have to; apologize for it; try to make it right. But as I've pointed out, the main organizations in this country have let us down every once in a while and end up in trouble with editors. So I don't maintain that an editor is salvation. There won't be editors in the future with the internet world, with citizen reporting just by the nature of it. That doesn't scare me. There's a notion that sticks and stones may break my bones, but words will kill me. I don't believe it. I get maligned every day on the news groups. I'm still standing. I still have a smile on my face. It's just the nature of this new thing. I mean, if I get defamed from Egypt, what do I do? Do I go to the World Trade Organization and ask for relief? This is the world we're going to be facing shortly, and I don't know exactly what the courts are going to do with this dynamic. I'm not too anxious about it however.

MR. HARBRECHT: Aren't you coarsening the public discourse? (Laughter.)

MR. DRUDGE: I hope not. You know, these questions are pretty tough, and I think if you directed this type of tough questioning to the White House, there'd be no need for someone like me, quite frankly. (Laughter/applause.) I have fun with what I do. A lot of it's smiles. A lot of it's "Look, Ma, I can dance." A lot of it's preempting other newspapers. I cover politicians the way the—I cover media people the way they cover politicians. I'm reporting Jeff Gerth may be breaking something in a couple of weeks, for example. That's fun stuff. That's a new paradigm. It's where the media is unchecked. It's where they're not the only game in town, where the media now is a guy with a 486 out in Hollywood. How did a story like Monica Lewinsky break out of a Hollywood apartment? What does that say about the Washington press corps? It just baffles me. I haven't come up with answers on that. (Applause.)

MR. HARBRECHT: I think Monica Lewinsky was from Hollywood, wasn't she? (Laughter.) How many sources do you require before posting an item?

MR. DRUDGE: Well, a little more than Bob Woodward's "Deep Throat" from time to time. (Laughter, scattered applause.) Sometimes I'll go with one person. The Loral worker who came forward and told me the encryption was missing from the satellite— the biggest nightmare scenario for defense types—I went with that one . . . [The New York Times fronted the missing encryption one month later.] What I do is a formula where I follow my conscience—and this is upsetting to some people—but I maintain the conscience is going to be the only thing between us and the communication in the future, now. And I'm very happy with my conscience.

MR. HARBRECHT: How many leaked stories do you get from mainstream journalists, and would you speculate on their motivation?

MR. DRUDGE: That's a good question, because what I've been doing lately is breaking news that's about to be broken, coverage of the coverage of the coverage. But that's where we are, since the media is so powerful. The media is comparable to government—probably passes government in raw power. A lot of the stories are internal. They leak it to me wanting to get attention, wanting to get that headline. More times than not, I will not give it to them. It has to get—has to raise my whiskers. It has to be a good headline. I'm a sucker for a good story. I go where the stink is. I'm a partisan for news. If you got a story, I'll be listening outside when we're done. (Soft laughter.)

MR. HARBRECHT: All right, you've got your hat on, and you seem to emulate in your dress and advocate in your presentation the good old days of the tabloids of the '20s and '30s. But does populism equal consistently good journalism?

MR. DRUDGE: I'll have to ask Tom Brokaw that. I don't necessarily think a populism means you're out defaming people left and right. A populism press is a press that cares about the country. Most of my sources are concerned citizens, in and out of government, who don't like the direction of the White House Press Office, for example. Or quite frankly, a lot of the people on the Hill aren't quite forthcoming answering questions. I reported a great story about a website that had been set up, had been registered "Friends of Al Gore PAC." The billing address they used for this PAC was 1600 Pennsylvania Avenue. Someone had registered a political action committee from the White House, using it as a billing address. This is a huge story. I had it exclusively. I guess mainstream press don't know how to work the internet and get the information. This is an example of a populous press. It's very concerning. That, to me, was violating quite a few laws. They said someone in the office had set it up, and they were told to bring it down, and it wasn't—bring it down. They changed the address eventually. I looked up the address. It was a graveyard in Denver. That's a populist press to me.

MR. HARBRECHT: Matt, what types of stories would fall into the category that you would not publish?

MR. DRUDGE: Hmm. There's quite a few stories I don't publish that come my way. For instance, specific descriptions on these Lewinsky tapes of the presidential anatomy, I'm not reporting. I've had it, I've held it back. [Author-reporter Jeffrey Toobin would later highlight the president's penis size in his '00 bestseller A Vast Conspiracy, Random House, $25.95.] This, to me, composed quite an interesting dilemma on a world stage, quite frankly. That is an example that I don't think furthers the story. That Phil Hartman may have met his wife through a prostitute doesn't necessarily interest me. I'm an advocate. I love public policy. Those are the types of stories that get me—get me typing. I also like to have fun. I like to do ratings and box office, just to show that it's not really about the product. It's more fun to talk about Godzilla than to watch it, for example. (Laughter.) So I don't have one straight category of things I rule out. I tend not to do drugs, I tend not to do serious stuff that would upset people in private lives. That's probably my criterion of drawing the line, which I get a lot of it. I simply hit the "delete" and keep moving. I get 10,000 e-mails a day. There's—odds are there's another morsel at the next click.

MR. HARBRECHT: Where does your money come from? Explain the economics of The Drudge Report. How do you make a living from a free website? (Scattered laughter.)

MR. DRUDGE: Richard Mellon Scaife is not my benefactor, if that's the question. (Scattered laughter.) I haven't made a penny off The Drudge Report. It's been free. For the four years I've been doing it now, the website is free. There's not advertising on it. [One year later, there would be.] It was a labor of love, it continues to be. I sell the column, I have sold the column, first to Wired magazine up in South Park, San Francisco, and now to AOL [a man can make the same living from his enemies as his friends—it's the new economy] and I've just been hired to do a TV show, made some money that way. [Legal terms of my separation with "Network" insist that I not disparage it.] But I didn't get into this for money . . . I still wear the same beat-up shoes I've had since the day I started this, still walk the same streets. So, that's—I think this is not a cash medium yet. There's probably quite a few people making money on the hype of it [see Nasdaq] but the actual application of it? Don't quite see it yet.

MR. HARBRECHT: I just have to call this to attention, because it's something that used to drive people crazy about Richard Nixon, and you just did it, which is you threw out a sort of juicy little tidbit about Phil Hartman here, saying, "but I don't really—I don't really have any interest in that kind of thing," when in fact that's exactly what is on your website all the time. And I call attention to it, because that's exactly the kind of thing that I think infuriates journalists about what you do. I wonder if you could comment.

MR. DRUDGE: Would you care to give me another example? I did not report the Phil Hartman thing on my website. Another example could help me.

MR. HARBRECHT: Well, you just threw out, as you throw out things on your website all the time. And it was—it was just put out there with no corroboration. Who—who reported that?

MR. DRUDGE: I think one of the syndicated magazines just reported that. [Globe tab, one week later.] But my question is, again, what headline on my website would you call in that category?

[Long Pause]

MR. HARBRECHT: Okay. Fair enough. (Applause).

MR. DRUDGE (sotto voce): I forgive you . . .

MR. HARBRECHT: Could you—could you succeed as a journalist, if you worked for an organization which required an accuracy rate of 100 percent, instead of 70 or 80 percent?

MR. DRUDGE: I don't know what organization that would be. (Scattered laughter.) (Applause.) I once gave a quote—you know, I do a lot of predictions. I have The Truman Show making $300 million. I once gave a quote that "Oh, I guess I'm 80 percent accurate, the body of my work." Newsweek magazine, and then Karen Breslau, who I happened to see in the courtroom—in the courthouse hallways—she's on the pay phone, she says, "Oh, Matt Drudge, my name's Karen Breslau." "Oh, I know you. You're the one who made up a quote on me." She—she reported Drudge is going to have trouble with his lawsuit, because his— he claims his sources are, quote, "Eighty percent reliable." I've never talked about the reliability of my sources. I said, "Karen, you made that up!" She shrugged her shoulders: "Whatever." This is—this is mainstream press . . . Now, if this is the standard—if this is the skyscraper up on Sixth Avenue that I want to dream about, I'd rather stay in my dirty Hollywood apartment. I just don't take what people give me. I tend to at least try to frame it with an angle that would consider both sides—provocative stuff.

MR. HARBRECHT: Why then don't you always call both sides when you report something?

MR. DRUDGE: I make it a point to call both sides. Unfortunately Mike McCurry is not taking my calls anymore. (Laughter.) It's just absolutely amazing that he—the White House has now refused all comment on anything I'm reporting. . . . That kind of stuff just rubs me the wrong way—and at their own peril—no comment.

MR. HARBRECHT: For someone who has been attacked by the mainstream press, your website provides easy links to all the establishment media. Why do you do that?

MR. DRUDGE: Well, because it's—to me it's—I started it with a place where readers could keep up—links to the various columnists. The links I have on my website I declare to be the most interesting people working in the business—all up and down—left, right and middle—I love to feature them. It's just a click away. You don't have to go through the front page—you go right to the column. A click away, you go to the AP Washington File—up to the minute. I started it as a lark. It built itself after I started collecting these names on the website. And it certainly has changed the way things are done—for the pedestrian anyway. And I've been told quite a few people are reading it—from the top level in government down—for access—for quick access, unfiltered access—a click to Helen Thomas's latest column, reintroducing a whole new generation to wire services and columnists—I love them all. So I don't consider myself an enemy of the press whatsoever, but I do consider myself to be an untrained D student who happened to get lucky, but who happens to know a few things, and he now has the ability to shout down the street, "Extra, Extra, This Just In."

MR. HARBRECHT: What advice would you give to others, such as Jennycam, who claim—who are out to find fame through the internet?

MR. DRUDGE: Well, you know, fame for fame's sake is—you know, always leaves a bad taste in my mouth. And you have to give them something they haven't heard. There has to be a reason they'll come to your website. If it's just made-up fantasies, why bother? You know, if I'm so bad and if I'm so useless and I'm just a gossip hound, why was Sidney Blumenthal reading me the night before his first day at the White House? I don't quite understand that. It seems to me I'd spend my time over at the New York Times, who gets everything right. Advice is to follow your heart and to do what you love. And I certainly am doing what I love. Again, I wrote The Drudge Report for one reader for a while—a couple of readers—5, 10, 15 readers. I had a thousand—the first couple of months I thought, oh, that peaked that out. Again, I'm up to these millions I never thought I'd see. And with the advent of Web TV and cable modems, I don't know where this is going. Sixty million readers? What is civilization going to do with the ability of one citizen—without advertisers, without an editor—to broadcast to that wide group of people? The First Lady says we need to rethink it. I say we need to embrace it. And it will take care of itself—it always has. It will get evened out.

MR. HARBRECHT: Here's a question that just came up. With all due respect, in the past half hour you have been inaccurate 8 to 10 times—about history, government, the media. You said there were no suits approved by a president, no profits in early newspaper and radio. Do you think journalists should have any minimum educational requirements?

MR. DRUDGE: Hmm, I've done—I guess I'm going to the wrong libraries, because I can't find any lawsuit—civil lawsuit approved by the president of the United States against a reporter. I can't find it. I'd like to have that information for my litigation—put it in the court papers. Again, I don't maintain that I am licensed or have credentials. I created my own. I don't know what the problem is with that. It seems to me the more freedoms we have the better off we are. And you know I don't have a problem with chaos and new invention and confusion. I'm sure in the early days of electricity it was absolutely chaotic. The early days of cars, the horse farmers probably said, "What are those things?" It's not where I come from. I'm much more optimistic—knowing liberty and freedom is the right way to go, knowing a new invention is afoot that is going to realize things beyond anything we dreamed of. I'm not that scared of it. But then again I'm not in elected office. You know, the president, the Congress, take [what I do] personally. They're just the first to come through this internet era. The person that sits in the Oval Office next will get my undivided attention.

MR. HARBRECHT: Are journalists obsolete who fail to include their e-mail addresses in their columns?

MR. DRUDGE: Well, you know, I'm getting so—that's a hit or miss. I mean, I would advise interaction, simply because you'll never know what you'll learn by offering an e-mail address . . . you'd be surprised what the average guy knows. Some of my best sources have turned out to be people who happened to be in the room that shouldn't have been in the room but who have come forward. I would provide as much contact with the public as you can. Again, I'm getting so much e-mail now I can't possibly read it. So it's a mixed blessing. But I would try to be as open as you can and offer an e-mail address—most of them do. I have correspondence with the top newspaper reporters in the business through e-mail, and it's a fun relationship—it's better than the phone. You could be doing other things at the same time.

MR. HARBRECHT: There were two recent episodes in our business where stories in the reporting of the Monica Lewinsky case, where newspapers put out pre-published stories online that turned out to be half-baked, frankly. Do you foresee a separation of media practices where future journalists accept more your style and methods, or accept the methods of appropriate journalism?

MR. DRUDGE: Appropriate? I guess you're referring to the Dallas Morning News story and the Wall Street Journal story. Mistakes are made. Mistakes are made all the time. I am not that alarmed by these mistakes. I think they tend to correct themselves. Just because they're on the internet doesn't mean they're less powerful, say, than if they are broadcast on CBS. I don't distinguish it. I don't think the rush to publish is any different from the rush to get it ready for the evening news. It's the same kind of rush. It's our history. Think about the Philadelphia newspaper that had 12 editions a day. What was that rush like? Probably a lot of sloppy stuff. But this is the kind of tradition we have. It's kind of sloppy. And, again, I don't advocate being sloppy, but that is our roots. . . . The problem I'm seeing immediately is if other Drudge Reports pop up—and they will—it is romantic to have one person running down the street screaming, "Extra, extra," but if you have a thousand it could start looking like an insane asylum. So if indeed we start having tens of thousands of people all reporting news, hundreds of channels reporting news, all the different cable channels—click, click, click—I think people will grow disinterested. But again, they'll rally around something else. So I leave this to the free marketplace. Every reader I have comes to me. I've never placed an ad. They read me because they want to. The vice president will log on, hit my website because he wants to, et cetera.

MR. HARBRECHT: Since when is the rationalization "We've always been sloppy" a justification for tarnishing a great institution? Does the right of every citizen to shout, "Extra, extra, this just in," outweigh maintaining a professional ethic of journalism?

MR. DRUDGE: Professional. You see, the thing is you are throwing these words at me that I can't defend, because I'm not a professional journalist. I am not paid by anyone. So you are shutting the door in my face again, and I don't quite understand what that's about, because that is not the facts. I can print something without an editor. This is where we are now. I don't know exactly why that's so scary. I again put my name on everything I write, unlike a few other columnists in this room. If I am here to defend what I am writing, why isn't that enough? Why isn't that enough as a freedom of press, the freedom of speech, to carry water? I think it is. I just don't throw out reckless stuff at all. I do great pains. There's been plenty of stories I have killed with problems attached to them. So I just don't buy that argument.

(Applause.)

MR. HARBRECHT: One more time: Where do you receive your funding? I wonder if you could address that one more time please.

MR. DRUDGE: It's not Richard Mellon Scaife. (Applause.) I had some money saved up from my gift shop days at CBS—a late bloomer. I have a small apartment, $600 a month rent. I drive a Metro Geo. I take the A Train sometimes when I'm coming out of New York to the airport. I don't need much money to do a start-up business like this. Anyone for any reason can launch a website—little or no money—internet connection, local phone. The modem lets you cover the world. The modem lets you read what's happening if there is an earthquake in Alaska seconds after it happens. I think that's fun and dramatic—for free—by a medium that was built by taxpayer money. So perfectly realized. Let the future begin.

(Applause.)

MR. HARBRECHT: Matt, thank you for coming into the lion's den today. (Applause.) I have a certificate of appreciation for you speaking at the National Press Club; "Reliable Sources," which is our 90th anniversary history of the National Press Club—(laughter)—till the end, till the end; and our chalice, the National Press Club mug.

MR. DRUDGE: Thank you.

MR. HARBRECHT: For our final question today, what is the biggest mistake you have made so far?

MR. DRUDGE: That's a really good question. I've made a few mistakes. Ever doubting my ability was my biggest mistake, because in the beginning I didn't think much that I had the right to report things. But I was wrong. Boy, was I wrong. Whenever I tend to think, you know, "Oh, I probably shouldn't be reporting on the president of the United States, respect the office." I respect the office so much I want to cover it. And you know I maintain who is telling more truth this summer, me or the president of the United States? (Applause.) So I don't have many regrets. I don't have many regrets. I don't have many regrets in that area, except for doubting that this was my God-given right as an American citizen, and embracing it, and saying liberty is just wonderful, thanks to the people who have come before me who have stood up for it. And thank you. (Applause.)

MR. HARBRECHT: I'd like to thank you for coming today, Mr. Drudge.

MR. DRUDGE: Sure.
(p. 11)

DRUDGE'S MOST-USED BOOKMARKS

http://www.stocksmartpro.com/ows-bin/owa/prologin.home
http: news.excite.com/other/reuters
[OBFUSCATED FOR SECURITY]
[OBFUSCATED FOR SECURITY]
[OBFUSCATED FOR SECURITY]
http://www.nytimes.com/info/contents/textpath.html
http://www.telegraph.co.uk
http://www.washtimes.com
http://www.washingtonpost.com
http://www.the-times.co.uk
http://www.nypostonline.com
http://www.hollywoodreporter.com
[OBFUSCATED FOR SECURITY]
http://www.variety.com
http://cloakroom.com/pubs/hotline/
http://web.lexis-nexis.com
http: nrstg1s.djnr.com/cgi-bin/DJInteractive
[OBFUSCATED FOR SECURITY]
http://www.newsday.com/ap/topnewsx.htm
gopher: wister.sbs.ohio-state.edu/
http: quake.wr.usgs.gov/cgi-bin/finger?quake@gldfs.cr.usgs.gov
http://edis.oes.ca.gov/bulletins/
http://www.showbizdata.com/contacts/dailybox.htm
http: uote.yahoo.com/intlmarkets

LETTERS TO THE EDITOR

#1
Matt,

<u>You are the Thomas Payne of our era!</u> You cut though the spin doctored, poll generated fog of lies cast by high paid pundits to expose the truth behind the crumbling ruins of our once proud democracy! The ghosts of such men as Jefferson, Lincoln, and Truman are with you. They have turned in their graves too long and now pull with you to let the people know what crimes are going on in the republic they made. If the conditions continue, and if economic failure opens the eyes of the population, it will be men like you on the barracades of a second American Revolution. <u>Don't let those of faint heart dampen your resolve to keep high the torch of truth for it is that illumination that keeps alive the hope of liberty.</u>

Richard Senate,

Ghost Hunter, author of *The Ghost Stalker's Guide to Haunted California* (shameless plug), Charon Press, Ventura, California (heart of Reagan Country), and Big Fan

(p. 22)

#2
My name is George Brown.

I live in the small town of Emmett, Idaho. But with the Drudge Report I'M IN THE HEAT OF POLITICS, WORLD EVENTS, CORRUPTION, HOLLYWOOD, SPIES, DISASTER'S ECT . . .

I'M ON AN EVEN PLAYING FIELD WITH THE BIG BOYS. I EVEN KNOW BEFORE THEY KNOW. <u>WHEN I'M INFORMED MY FAMILY IS INFORMED. MY FRIENDS ARE INFORMED.</u>
<u>WHEN YOU'RE WELL INFORMED, YOU MAKE WELL</u>

INFORMED DECISIONS. drudgereport.com KEEPS ME
INFORMED!!!
THANKS MATT
(p. 22)

#3
Hi,
My name is Karen (name change to protect my identity), and
I'm a Drudgaholic. Yes, <sigh> I'm addicted to the Drudge
Report. It started very innocently, really, with the internet surge I,
too, got online. Checked out some search engines. Spent time
in the chat rooms. But it was there, in the chat rooms, that my
problem began.

Everyone was talking about the Drudge Report.

"Have you been to the Drudge Report?" "Did you read what
Drudge said today?" Anyone without the latest scoop from
Drudge, well, they were left out. Uninformed. IGNORED! <gag>

So, you see, I HAD to see what all the fuss was about.

There was no warning label. No one spoke of a 12 step
treatment program. Late night refreshing of the Drudge Report,
just to be sure you have the latest scoop while your family is fast
asleep. I just didn't know what I was getting myself into.

And it didn't just stop at just getting the story. NO! That
wouldn't have been so bad. But then, needing better debate
ammo, the link obsession began. "Does the New York Post have
a story on it." "oh my G-d, I can't believe he did THAT with a
cigar . . ." "I wonder what Ann Coulter, George Will, Cal Thomas,
Thomas Sowell, Walter Williams, David Limbaugh . . . . the
Washington

Times . . . . WorldNetDaily . . . . . . Lucianne . . . .
oh . . . JACKPOT! THE JEWISH WORLD REVIEW . . . .
and on and on and on . . . . don't forget the liberal spin
(best source is The New York Times) . . . . . one must anticipate
what the other side will say; the parcing, the lynching of the
messengers, define "sex," define "is."

It's Drudge's fault really. They're all there. They're easy. My
life is flashing before my eyes, but . . . . . hmmm, I wonder if
anyone has a story on that . . . . ?

PLEASE, SOMEONE . . . . . . HELP ME!
(p. 23)

#4
Dear Matt,
In plain terms, you're my hero. You showed the elitist snobs of the establishment media that one man with a dream, a PC, and perseverance can scoop them on a regular basis and be right as often as they are. Sometimes more often than they are.

You also proved that the most important component of a website is information. Not bells and whistles, not the latest RealPlayer plug in, not bandwidth-clogging animation, but information.

You, Matt, represent what the media should be: tenacious, disrespectful, honest, entertaining, and unstoppable in your pursuit of the truth.

Screw the networks and their holier than thou attitude. Drudge! Long may he reign!
Rick Medlin
(p. 24)

#5
Matt,
As a certified info-maniac, I have to compliment you on your web site. You not only break the stories, you provide links to sources so people can find out the facts for themselves. This is an invaluable service in a society that is polluted with "news sources" that are actually opinion outlets. Many times I have heard your web site quoted as a source for "news." The only problem is, they cite your story three or four days after you have printed.

I have discovered the only way to stay on top of the news, at work or home, is through your site. I make extensive use of the links to wire services, major news outlets, and of course your breaking news. I have a background in broadcast journalism, but left the field because I saw the way the industry was headed. I did not fit in with the tabloid news media types. I wanted to be a reporter. Your site is forcing the media to evaluate the "infotainment" path it has taken. You have, can, and will continue to change the way news is reported.

Respectfully,
Jim Sullivan
Broomfield, CO
(p. 24)

#6

I first learned of the Drudge Report in a newspaper article a few years ago. That weekend I found it online. I left it on the screen while I did other work on the computer, occasionally checking back to see if the information was updated during the day. <u>On one check the headline spoke of Princess Diana having been in a car wreck.</u> I went to my TV and checked CNN but there was nothing. After about 5 minutes there was a Breaking News item about the accident. I was amazed. . . . this guy in a one-bedroom apartment in LA had beat the major networks to the story. And I had no idea how long the story had been posted before I had checked back to the Drudge Report and reloaded it. I went back to work on my computer and a while later updated Drudge. Now he was reporting that the Princess had died. Again I went to the TV. Although the accident was now on all the channels, it was another 15 minutes before her death was suggested, let alone confirmed. Thereafter I made the Drudge Report my Home Page. Some weeks later Drudge Headlined the rumors about Sidney Blumenthal. Less than 24 hours later Drudge's top headline retracted the story. I thought at that time how responsible this reporter was. Unlike a major newspaper that screams headlines for days on end and then prints a tiny box on, say, page 8 retracting the story, Matt Drudge devoted as much space to his retraction as he did to the original story. The subsequent hoopla by the regular media denouncing the Drudge Report on this matter is so ironical and, to say the least, hypocritical. Finally, I had spent a long time trying to find a full list of AP stories and new articles by various columnists. The Drudge Report has a listing of many major newspapers and columnists that are now a click away, as well as the AP, Reuters and UPI wire reports. Matt Drudge's Report has the best news summaries and the fastest breaking news service anywhere, on the internet or when compared to any other media. It is also the most accurate and HONEST source of news of which I'm aware. The Drudge Report remains and will continue to remain my Home Page.

Best regards,
Chuck Judge
Los Angeles, CA
(p. 24)

#7

Dear Matt, I have been online since 1997 . . . and yet even today I still find new services, tips, tricks, twists amd turns that leave me evermore enchanted with this great medium. I characterize you as a virtual information tourguide as well as digital commentator. One of the most vivid memories I have of you to date was your appearance on "Politically Incorrect." I have never seen Bill Maher more beside himself with hatred toward a guest. The origin of this anger wasn't because of your hand in the Monica Lewinsky/Bill Clinton scandal. It was due to a younger and more intelligent "cyber punk" who had achieved more in his six years than Mr. Maher ever has in his whole lifetime. They are not so much angry at you for WHAT you did . . . everyone knows that Bill Clinton is a cad and that he truly doesn't deserve the office. They are mad because of HOW you did it. I mean come on . . . <u>who ever heard of someone getting famous because of the internet ;o)</u>

Dan Gettelfinger
Cincinnati, OH
(p. 28)

#8

I am an American who spends a large amount of my time outside the United States. I also happen to be a bit of a news junkie. Every day I log on to the Drudgereport to see what is going on in the world. I always look forward to seeing the latest tidbit of info Drudge has reported that the "big guys" miss. <u>The fact that the mainstream media takes its cheap shots at Drudge should be worn as a badge of honor.</u> Though I fully realize that not everything posted on the Drudgereport is fully accurate, my guess is that his record is at least as good as the mainstream media. Furthermore, the thing that seems to gall the big boys the most is the fact that they don't get to decide for us what is newsworthy, the Lewinsky case being the most obvious example. Fundamentally, I don't believe in the notion of unbiased journalism. It's a lofty ideal, but like many others, it can never be attained. How is it that Roger Clinton gets the red carpet treatment in North Korea or Hillary gets booed every time she is in public and nobody ever hears about it? I prefer a style of adversarial journalism whereby the media proudly wears its prejudices on its sleeve. At least then I can compare the articles written on both sides of the argument and decide for myself which I feel is the strongest. Attempts at unbiased journalism tend to be editorial pieces carefully crafted to sound objective. I love the links Drudge provides to writers and publications on both sides of the aisle. Every once in a while I like to read the latest from Molly Ivins or Hillary just to reaffirm my own beliefs (and for a bit of comic relief). The Drudgereport is the most democratic news site that I am aware of. I can find anything I want from the AP wires to the latest editorial by Walter Williams to the Bloomberg financial news all from one website. Equally, I could find links to Salon Magazine, the New Republic, or the National Enquirer if I'm in the mood for fiction. Keep up the good work and give 'em hell.

Stan Falk
Thailand
(p. 33)

#9
I can't stand your political attitudes or your fast and loose way with "journalism." Nor can I stand how addicted I am to your site and how much I love it. Keep up the good . . . I mean bad . . . work. For better or for worse, you're making history— and it's fun helping you do it (by adding to the number of hits you get each day).

P.J. Sierra
(p. 36)

#10
Matt,
From the moment I discovered the DRUDGE REPORT, I felt as if I found a diamond mine of information. In my own mind, it was a one stop shop to find today's news and what's going on.

Know how someone sends cards for all occasions? I sent more of DRUDGE REPORT's website to everyone that I met, so that they could start off the day as I did. INFORMED.

Saying "Thank You" is never enough to you, Matt Drudge. You deserve some kind of award that has never been given before because you are in a class by yourself. You are not only unique. You are courageous. You live your convictions. You are the journalist's journalist but have never been credited for the enormous work that you do. You seek TRUTH and it does come across to those of us who are TRUTH SEEKERS.

Thank You, Matt Drudge for the DRUDGE REPORT. We owe you a debt of gratitude that could never be repaid. You are a true patriot. You are a wonderful citizen. You are one of my heroes.

I Love You . . . . Matt Drudge. You make my day begin. . . . .
Rosalie Boyle
Reno, NV
(p. 41)

#11

Internet news is provided in two forms: The first is filtered, illustrated and spun according to the site, and the second is the Drudge Report. In a class by itself, the Drudge Report makes ALL news available ALL the time. From the AP and the UPI to the writings of well-known columnists and links to a huge number of web news sources, the Drudge Report provides instant access to current information which other news sources pick through, sort and filter. Without the graphics it loads quickly. The headlines allow the reader to scan quickly through major news items and get on with the day.

Radio and TV news sources (including Rush Limbaugh) repeat throughout the day what I've already learned in the morning from the headlines listed on the Drudge Report. Keep it rolling, Matt!

Matt Walters

Married, father of one, Los Angeles native, currently a Ph.D. candidate in structural engineering at the University of Illinois at Urbana-Champaign

(p. 54)

#12

Dear Matt,

As a graduate student studying journalism, I often had to sit in classes full of pompous academics who laughed at me because I believed what you wrote on your site. "The internet is not a reliable source of information," one professor admonished. "Anyone can write anything. Don't believe what you read." Others rolled their eyes when I cited your site.

Then Monicagate broke. Nobody wanted to believe it was true until they read it in Time magazine. But you proved what I knew all along—that people who have a nose for news, not bloated corporations, are the real journalists of this country. Damn the mainstream. There's more corruption in the corporate media than our founding fathers would have ever predicted. So thanks for your site. You are the embodiment of the American way. Keep fighting the money men and bringing us great news.

Stacy Holmstedt
(p. 55)

#13
Dear Matt Drudge:
Few people today are aware of an early 20th century intellectual, journalist, and author named Charles Fort, who collected bits of arcane news and credible but startling information that Fort called "damned data" because Science would not accept these incidents within their rigid journals. Today, you, Matt Drudge, seem to be treading some of the same ground. Your page is visited by revolutionary scientists, cryptozoologists, hominologists, and forteans who watch the wire services for hints of everything from sightings of Yeti in the Himalayas to reports of enigmatic ice falls in Spain and Italy. Your interest in phemonema has not gone unnoticed by a silent group of scholarly skeptics and academic anomalists worldwide that investigate such short-term events. You are to be congratulated for going outside the mainstream subjects to shine a bit of light on what may be intriguing future discoveries.

I certainly know in my world, on the internet, in my university work, and with the articles, columns, and books I write, your site is extremely important. The first place I go to read, every hour or so, is The Drudge Report. Thank you for being there at the breaking edge of all of our tomorrows.

Sincerely,
Loren Coleman, MSW
professor, cryptozoologist, writer, filmmaker
University of Southern Maine
(p. 64)

#14

Drudge,

<u>I'll never forget being informed about the Lewinsky scandal on the Drudge Report before it broke on the national news.</u> For me, that was my first taste of the real power of the internet. It transformed me from a timid internet tinkerer, to a ravenous internet newshound. Thanks Matt Drudge!!!!! Don't stop.

Matt Sweitzer
Pickerington, OH
(p. 68)

#15

As one who also studies society in my work as a university sociology professor, I find the DRUDGEREPORT to be refreshing and extremely useful. I need to know what is happening rather quickly, or my students will inform me. The DRUDGEREPORT seems to get information early and offers it for public consideration. <u>I often read things on the DRUDGEREPORT that places like CNN report a day or two later. I find myself saying, "I knew that yesterday."</u> The collection of links to other news sources and people is also helpful in my work. The DRUDGEREPORT put news together in an exciting and welcome package that no other source is doing. I sure hope the art of "drudge" is being taught in journalism schools. I am addicted to the DRUDGEREPORT as a unique information source and I regularly recommend it to students in my social problems course.

Jeffrey W. Riemer, Ph.D.
Professor of Sociology
(p. 70)

#16

OK, as per your request, here's my letter:

Much has been said about whether or not Matt Drudge is a "journalist" or not, and this is something you have to decide for yourself. But the real value in the Drudge Report website is not in his opinion pieces, but rather the links Matt provides to stories that other journalists have filed on the web. Stories of the unusual. Stories that have been buried by the liberal-leaning mass media. Hell, even stories that contradict other stories that he's also linked to. Stories that make you THINK FOR YOURSELF, and question the wisdom of simply believing everything you read.

Matt Drudge shows us that a steady diet of CNN, or your local newspaper, or however it is you receive your daily news, is not enough. He encourages us, by going out and digging up these offbeat and sometimes politically incorrect stories, to in turn seek out more information, to not just blindly trust the smiling newscaster who assures us that he/she will tell us everything we need to know (and therefore anything he/she does not tell us isn't something we need to know). He casts a strong spotlight on the traditional media, and shows us just how biased they can be. He encourages us to ask questions, to not just ACCEPT what we're told but to wonder why we're being told this, and how it will REALLY affect us. And he's had a strong effect. Stories that he has featured have later, begrudgingly, received "traditional" media coverage . . . coverage they wouldn't have received had Matt Drudge not lit a fire under a few asses. Is Matt Drudge a journalist? I can't answer that question . . . but if he is not, then I say, let there be fewer journalists, and more Matt Drudges. We've seen the value in having just one of him. :-)
Joey Lindstrom
Calgary, Alberta, Canada
(p. 71)

#17
Look, up on the screen, it's black, it's white, it's read all over—DRUDGE REPORT!
How did we survive before we discovered that we could go to the Matt for issues that plague our society, lift our spirit and scare the crap out of us? Now that we have discovered the super powers that this man of steel (or is it spiel) can offer us, we find ourselves at our "favorite place" on a daily routine.

Is this addictive? We don't recognize anything abnormal about needing and wanting to Drudge through our news. Of course we could have the Lois Lane Syndrome; she never recognized Superman when he put glasses and a hat on his head. And speaking of hats, why don't more newsmen start wearing them?

Frankly, I don't trust anyone to give me the latest scoop if they are not wearing a Walter Winchell hat. How can they possibly report with a naked head? It's obscene.

There is a very valuable and serious side to the DRUDGE REPORT. The news is more powerful than a locomotive and Matthew Drudge has been able to leap tall stories in a single bound. His fight for truth and justice is the epitome of the American way of reporting. Far away in other lands his skills are recognized and his site ranks in the top 10 of the entire world as being important. When danger lurks or politicians are jerks, he puts his hat on and becomes DRUDGEMAN, typing away at any hour and always mindful of his power.

By day, mild-mannered and easy-going Matthew Drudge works for the planet, gathering information while everyone recognizes that he is the same strong, confident and talented Matt Drudge by night. That's when the glasses and hat go on and his super powers appear. Through cyberspace he flies delivering the news, undaunted by the bullets that make up the headlines.

Superman, mom's apple pie and Drudge are American icons at their best. Look! Out in cyberspace!

It's a word, it's the news, it's . . . DRUDGE REPORT!

C.L.

(p. 84)

#18

In a last-ditch effort, a desperate father insists on buying his underachiever son a computer. "Yeah," says the son. "And what am I going to do with that?"

What did Matt Drudge do?

He changed the course of American history. He proved that the truth always matters. He 1000% justified his father's belief in his potential. And he showed that a good idea plus the freedom to pursue it are still the living heart of the American Dream.

I know the Liberal media would love us to believe that their *fair-haired boys & girls* are what the Founding Fathers had in mind when they wrote and spoke about freedom. Thank you, Matt Drudge, for using your "Drudge Report" to demonstrate to the Media Elites and to the world exactly why the Founding Fathers gave us freedom—and why they so wisely refused to leave power only in the hands of the anointed.

(P.S. Anyone who loves the "Drudge Report" just has to see the video of Matt Drudge at the National Press Club on June 2, 1998. Beg for it, borrow or steal—but get this tape! Brilliant, straightforward, unpretentious, completely himself and astonishingly gracious in a bravura performance before a truly hostile audience, Drudge never loses his cool . . . and he gets in a few zingers in his own (truly) inimitable style. Plus, you get to hear Drudge himself describe his early years, how he got his start and what he thinks about how the internet will affect the media. An American—and Conservative—classic!)
Patrice Robertie
Arlington, MA
(p. 90)

#19
I discovered the Drudge Report a couple of years ago when I finally got on line. Since then, it has been my home page and gets several hits a day, either from my home or my work computer. It's the only credible, reliable source I've found for news that's way ahead of the mainstream media. When I would be asked "Did you hear about—fill in major or minor news event of your choice?" most times I can honestly say "Sure, I read about that on Drudge's page yesterday."

Don't know how Matt does it, but *he certainly does his homework and manages to publish the real story what seems like ages ahead of anyone else.* I suspect this is what our founding fathers had in mind when they talked about freedom of the press.
Toni Storey
(p. 92)

#20
Dear Mr. Drudge,
I must have heard about your site 2 years ago or so. Since then it has literally become my morning paper, waiting on my virtual doorstep. I love it. I also wish I'd thought of it!

The Drudge Report has all the elements of a great paper. It offers great columns from my favorite editorialists—William Buckley and George Will. It offers funny stories from around the world, whether it be a wacky science experiment or a 15 pound

baby or some such thing—all very entertaining. And of course the links to the AP, UPI, and other press sources is a great example of how the internet is breaking down the barriers between citizens and information. When I first discovered your site, I read with interest the transcript from your National Press Club appearance. I am a C-Span user (not quite a junkie—or am I in denial???) and have watched many such events. I was very impressed with what you had to say. I continue to see the old gatekeepers (Cronkite, Donaldson, Koppel) wailing and moaning because the unwashed masses now can publish their own news. It is power lost for them. All the better for us, I say. So, in closing, keep it up. I don't have to agree with you to enjoy your product. Hell, it's free!!! You do a great job and I hope to read your report with my morning coffee for years to come.
Sincerely,
Seth Fleishman
(p. 95)

#21
Matt Drudge,
Since the first appearance of your web-site on the internet, people have been seeking you out in droves. Those who want the inside story on breaking news contact you early. <u>Those who would impugn your veracity besmirch you continuously</u>. Those who run from the contents of your coverage espy you from afar. <u>What a paradoxical bunch of voyeurs!</u> To each his own.

As a renegade journalist, you have maintained exceptional standards for any and all who would visit. Your savoir faire has been refreshing, especially in this day and age of "pocket book" journalism. The stories you break draw immediate interest and create discussions throughout the world. You're a lightning rod for news commentators and political hacks alike. You've kept us linked to valuable sources and persons across the globe.

As we close out the last year of this Millennium, I wish to personally thank you for being at the top of my Bookmarks— always there and always salient. There you have it: The opinion of a Florida Redneck that values your investigative services.
"Luther K. Lunchbucket"
Panama City, FL
(p. 96)

#22
Dear Matt,
I have come to the conclusion that the one thing, above all the other reasons for the success of your news service, is that it is an interactive place where people can come and talk to each other and discuss the news of the day or to just sit quietly in the background and listen to what others are saying. <u>It reminds me of the days of the "front porch."</u> You may or may not have lived during the front porch era (being only forty-two, I barely caught the last act), but you have no doubt heard of it; ordinary people at the end of a hard day's work would gather outside after dinner on the front porch or steps with their neighbors and fill each other in on what was happening in their community and the rest of the world.

It strengthened the bond between neighbors and produced a well informed citizen. And then the community killers air conditioner and TV were invented; everybody quit going outside and we basically sealed ourselves off and lost meaningful contact with each other and then the internet was created; and you, Mr. Matt Drudge, invited everyone across America to come sit on your front porch and talk or listen to what was happening in our little world. And come they t may not be as serene as sitting outside with a cool gentle breeze blowing across your face or hearing the thunder booming off in the distant as you cross swords on a topic with a neighbor of a differing opinion, but I'll take it.

The Drudge Report, just like the front porch, is strengthening the bond between neighbors and is producing a well informed citizen.
Bravo!
Michael Willis (Navy/Retired)
Valrico, FL
(p. 97)

#23
Dear Mr. Drudge,
My children are tired of me telling them, "This is not the same country I grew up in." As Balint Vazsonyi explains in his book "America's Thirty Years War—Who's Winning?," if you place a frog directly into a pot of hot water, it will jump out. But if you

place a frog in a pot of cold water which you gradually heat up, it will remain oblivious to being boiled. A subtle, insidious transformation has gradually taken place in our society, and only in retrospect might it be possible to place matters into proper perspective.

Your website has served as a perspectivizing catalyst because it facilitates freedom. There are useful links readily available to accommodate people from any political persuasion. It offers a virtual bazaar of ideas, resources, and perspectives. Most importantly, it does not underhandedly influence people regarding what they should be thinking about. It allows the reader the freedom to evaluate the merits of information available.

This is in significant contradistinction to where most Americans these days get their information these days—from TV network and cable news programs. Overflowing with the phoney aura of credibility and knowledgeable insight, network news anchors are powerfully influential. Although they may be able to legitimately claim that they do not tell people what to think and that they do their best to provide "balance" and "objectivity," they rarely provide sufficient perspective. They are guilty of selective abstraction; presenting only tiny parts of complex stories often fueled by innuendo. They do a terrible job of presenting important matters in a fair context. Worst of all, and missing from most people's awareness, is the fact that every single time a commentator utters the simple phrase, "So the question is . . . ," he or she is framing the issue for public consumption—dictating to a captive audience what it is they should be thinking about. Armed with absolutely no accountability whatsoever for how inordinately influential they are, this makes them incredibly powerful. As a consequece, the United States of America today is inundated with masses of pseudoenlightened people totally oblivious to how vulnerable they are to elitist, sanctimonious, propoganda-pimping "journalists." I have watched and read scathing criticisms of you by many of these self-appointed "journalists," and am stunned by how absolutely full of themselves they are. I guess we can never go back to the nineteen fifties when commentators just presented the news. But your website allows us all to find out what the news is, and provides the means for each reader to be his or her own judge. That is real education. That is real freedom of the press.

Thank you, Mr. Drudge.

Sincerely,

Alan N. Miller

(p. 99)

#24

Hail, Media-meister Matt! I heard your name mentioned somewhere and I logged on. This was before the Monica/Clinton scandal so, thanks to you, I was front row center for your amazing reports. I now log on daily to get my news and forget the old fossils on the soon to be extinct mainstream media. The success of your report proves to everyone with a brain that the mainstream media has been spoon feeding us pap when all we want is the plain and simple truth. May your reign be long and prosperous!

Sincerely,

Suzanne Lamonte

(p. 99)

#25

Dear Mr. Drudge:

I believe it was early in 1996 that my wife and I were having breakfast out with some close friends. (We try to meet with them every Wednesday for breakfast and good fellowship.) The subject always gets around to politics and we were asked if we had ever visited your web site. We hadn't then, but have sure contributed to the hits on your site since.

I have both IE and Netscape browsers. It makes no difference which one I am using, I bring up your site "http://www.drudgereport.com" first thing. I am retired and you will notice I said "I." While my wife is still sacked in, I hit the internet every morning for the day's news (around 6:00 AM). After reading your Alerts, Reports, Flashing Lights, Breaking News, Headlines, etc., I use your site for virtually all of my surfing the internet. It is amazing how often I view news stories on your site the day before it appears in our local newspaper.

My wife has her own computer, a laptop, and she may only get on the internet every two or three days but she always hits

"Drudge" first. You have made it easy for <u>two old folks</u> to keep up with what is going on out there! Don't Take Any Prisoners!!!
  Sincerely,
  Ronald Powers
  Edmond, OK
  (p. 99)

  #26
  Dear Matt—
  Greetings in Christ.
  Just a note to say thanks and keep up the good work.+AKA-I've been checking the Drudge Report for a few years now, I don't know how long but probably three years or so. For over two years my normal operating procedure when logging on to the Net is to click on "Drudge" and "get mail." As Senior Minister of St. Stephen's Presbyterian Church in Central Auckland, New Zealand, I've often used ideas generated from your reports for sermon topics.+AKA- I also do a monthly column in a community newspaper which your reports aid in idea and fact generation. I realize you're not perfect (neither am I—or anyone else for that matter) and that your detractors often focus on your few slip-ups; however it seems to me that you are quick, bold, and have integrity. I like and trust your reporting, and I appreciate the breadth of reports—from the biggies to the <u>"make you laugh out loud"</u> ones. Keep it up! Don't let the "powers that be" (in the physical helm) get you down, and when things get rough turn to the POWER THAT IS (Father, Son and Holy Spirit).
  Thanks and God's Blessings
  Dick Holland (Rev)
  (p. 107)

  #27
  I started accessing Drudgereport daily during the Monica investigation and have kept it up since then, usually making several hits during the US evening to early morning hours as items are added during the California late morning to evening hours.
  <u>Drudge discovered a novel paradigm for news distribution,</u> without the need for the print or broadcast infrastructures, in

particular without the professional staff. This freedom allows the one-man shop to complete with multinationals; it also explains the different rules he could follow, providing services that used to be off limits. We can compare the Monica chain of events with the Y2K chain of events; discussions of Y2K in chat rooms a few years back gradually mushroomed into a world wide scare, with consequence well in excess of its substance, partly because it tapped into the superstitious fears of the new Millennium. Monica would probably have been quickly forgotten if the scandal had not tapped into the existing Paula Jones suit and the Whitewater investigation, allowing two previously separate legal cases to merge into something greater than the sum of its parts.

The internet, with its tentacles into homes and offices all over the world, provides a link system allowing events to blow up more quickly and widely than it had been possible before. What part did it play in the Asian financial crisis, when investors, previously rushing in, often into poorly regulated markets with inadequate economic capabilities, all rushed out together? How much use did the Seattle and Davos protestors make, and plan to use for the future expansion of their protest movement, the internet?

Matt Drudge, by showing that gossip by net is a powerful social tool, has probably laid the path for many insurgents of the new century.

Chung-Kwong Yuen,
Professor of Computer Science,
National University of Singapore
(Author of *Leninism, Asian Culture and Singapore*)
(p. 125)

#28
Matt,
I just wanted you to know how you changed my life and the internet. Six years ago when you started the DRUDGE REPORT, the web was a collection of static pages written by college students and corporations. Those companies that did have pages consisted of brochures transformed to HTML.

The DRUDGE REPORT transformed the web into an active

medium and helped create Internet Time. There is no news cycle in cyberspace, so that a news story can not be buried in a Friday night news release. News is now just as important at 1 AM as at 5 PM for the evening news.

Politicians have had to change the way that they do business. They must now have instant replies written before it is needed. They know that they can no longer hide, the world is watching and talking in cyberspace.

The DRUDGE REPORT changed my life because it brought the news and insights direct to me without filters, whenever, wherever I wanted to read it. Matt brings the worlds of Hollywood, Washington, and the World all together in one place with his view on its meaning. He tears back the gloss and shows the world the real truth. He examines the spin and slows it down long enough to see straight through it. My opinion of politics and business are eternally changed by the DRUDGE REPORT and made me be more vigilant in seeking the truth and and not being fooled by press releases and 22 minute evening news reports. Thanks, Matt, for bringing the DRUDGE REPORT to the World and me.

Larry Riley
Plainsboro, NJ
(p. 125)

#29
Dear Matt,

It has been a long time coming for a forthright alternative to the mainstream media. American News has gone the way of sport teams in my opinion. First, players left teams and followed the money. Second, teams avoided players and got fined. Now we have spoiled millionaires being paid by adolescent billionaires. I never follow them, seldom watch them, making me an absent enthusiastic spectator.

The news did the same thing. First the Networks cover only their own agenda. Second, Newspapers seldom break a story anymore. Third, Talk Radio cons you into calling and just when you have something to say, they have no time left for you to say it! Well, I scarcely read the papers, sporadically listen to the radio and in no way watch the National News.

I am an American who loves our freedoms, and I refuse to salute anyone who thinks our government needs to be replaced until they can show me a better one to replace it. It is not a matter of hating the media, rather they just lost my respect based upon their own inane actions. Therefore, I am proof that the first amendment lives in spite of an expiring National Monopoly of the Media Elite that existed until 1994 when the Drudge Report was born. All of the sudden, we now know the National Enquirer breaks stories that campaign spinners called lies, and now are being sued. Grimly, Newsweek loses a scoop because it preferred to hide facts instead of report them. Ultimately, News organizations are all changing because of what the Drudge Report has actualized: "One common place for all people to read all points of views unedited." Consequently, I am more informed today because of Drudge. I can now see through the pimping pencil pushers' poetic license for privately owned publishers' propaganda purposes. No Newspaper captures my eyes until my computer boots to Drudge. No Radio Talk Show reaches my ears unless I check Drudge. Finally, no Television News Reader gets my attention period because I can get real details at the Drudge Report. Drudge has no equal to date. The Drudge Report is faster, more accurate and offers a more objective perspective on all subjects. More importantly, I trust what I read because Drudge reports retractions. This is why the National Media will never again dominate the news, misuse the truth, and get away with reporting just parts of a story. They don't know it yet, but they are as antiquated as horses on our streets. Oh, you'll see one once in a while, but you don't respect them, and you just grow tired of their triviality that amounts to advertised manure. In closing, your invitation said anyone may become famous by writing you a letter. I have never been interested in fame. I am just looking for one place where I can expect to find all the news in totality. The Drudge Report does just that, better than any place on the internet, and in the known universe!

Respectfully submitted,
J. J. Janos, III
(p. 140)

#30

Matt—

I communicated with you two years ago about Loral Corporation <u>regarding technology transfers to China</u>. You pursued that story, and made it a part of American history. I also told the story to my brother-in-law, who works for a major American news daily, and at the time was the White House reporter for that news daily. He ignored the story, while it helped make you the most important journalist of the past ten years. (He didn't so much want to ignore the story, as knew it wouldn't play.)

I can talk bluntly about this because my brother has left Loral, and so faces no consequences. The biggest story of this decade of prosperity is the willingness of our nation to spend it—in all directions—without real thought as to the consequences to us and to future generations. We may all get rich, or wise, or even better than we are. But I fear the future more now than ever, because the means of human destruction are increasingly pervasive.

Regards,

Michael

(p. 140)

#31

Dear Matt,

I have been on the net for about 5 years. I had first heard of your site when Rush Limbaugh referred to it in one of his broadcasts. A few keystrokes later I was at your site. Shortly after I discovered your site I made it my home page. It was clear during the Clinton impeachment that you had inside information. It was also clear that you were correct on everything you reported. You were also well ahead of the rest of the media. <u>It was really amazing that ABC, CBS, CNN and NBC with all of their vast resources could not keep up with you.</u> That is why I changed my home page to http://www.drudgereport.com and still have it as my home page today. I thought after Clinton got away with lying you might just be a one trick pony. I was wrong. Today I visit the Drudge Report several times a day. When the dirt is flying I rely on the Drudge Report. What really amazes me is I almost never go to any of the "big network" sites. CNN.com has never been entered into my browser. ABC.com is used a few times. MSNBC.com—why bother.

Thanks for being online and on time and on target.
Kyle Wesley
Dallas, TX
(p. 146)

#32

I live in the Republic of the Fiji Islands.

Keeping up with news and current affairs from this isolated corner in the Pacific Ocean used to be frustrating.

The internet has changed this and I find the Drudge Report to be an excellent doorway to the whole World.

Not just that though. Looking through your www.drudgereport.com website I am constantly reminded that the internet is a more level playing field than any other media channel. And in my mind that is the essence of internet media. That people are looking for a familiar face out there amidst the endless content. Coming from Matt Drudge makes it seem more personal.

Where does it go from here?
Cheers,
Ian Collingwood
Director of Marketing
Sunflower Airlines, Nadi Airport, Fiji
(p. 162)

#33

Matt Drudge did something that hasn't been done since Adolph Ochs bought the New York Times: He democratized the media. Whether you like what he chooses to cover or not, it is undeniable that Drudge has impact. And he didn't build this impact by buying up TV stations like Rupert Murdoch or Ted Turner, or by consolidating papers into an empire, like the Gannett Chain.

Ironically, Drudge used the newest medium to resurrect the oldest truth of journalism: That a good reporter doesn't need a name or a hairdo or a degree from Columbia J-school. Reporters just need to be driven and resourceful, with a pinch of chutzpah thrown in for flavor.

Because of Drudge, anybody can be their own news service

today. This certainly brings up questions of credibility and competence, but for the most part, it is an excellent thing. GE and Disney and the other oligarchs that now run the press have reason to quake in their thousand-dollar boots at this onslaught of Internet Spartacuses.
Peter Orvetti
Orvetti Political Report
(p. 163)

#34
Dear Mr. Drudge:
I am Nathan V. Hoffman, a Los Angeles attorney specializing in Juvenile and Family Law. As a nearly daily reader of your website, I have nothing but the highest praise for what you have been able to accomplish in six short years via the internet. You have opened the door for "the masses" who have felt disillusioned by the "elite" type of journalism promulgated by the New York/Los Angeles Times crowd. Mr. Drudge you have done a great public service for the nation by opening the news media world to anyone with a PC or MAC capable of accessing the internet. You have inspired citizens from throughout this great nation, and indeed globally, to feel they too can help change the world by becoming reporters in their own right if they so desire. In other words, the "common man" now has a model in the DRUDGE REPORT which proves he too can make an impact and difference on issues of the day via the WWW. Is this not the essence of a true and "full participatory democracy" in our modern age? Our "Founding Fathers" would be pleased.
By having a website that allows your readers instant access to a myriad of links to a wide array of diverse reporters and wire services, you have demonstrated the most important characteristics of being a good journalist . . . BEING IMPARTIAL, UNBIASED, and TRUTHFUL. Moreover, by breaking stories ahead of the "mainstream media" (most notably the Monica Lewinsky scoop which nearly toppled the Presidency), you have proven to be the "People's Reporter," on alert for news other conventional media outlets ignore or intentionally overlook. It is always refreshing to read your hardnosed, no holds barred, column where TRUTH is given the highest premium, no matter where it leads.

Thank you MATT DRUDGE for having the vision to realize the importance of opening the world of print media journalism to "individual citizens" through the internet. There is no doubt that your pioneering efforts will be recognized as a watershed moment in journalistic history as we enter the brave new world of the 21st Century.

Sincerely,
NATHAN V. HOFFMAN, Attorney at Law
(p. 163)

#35
Your web-site has provided our family the first truly global news source, allowing us to circumvent the standard fare offered by the establishment print and electronic media. So long to newspaper subscriptions and CNN. Just for the record, we're a non-traditional family. My wife is Hispanic, first generation college educated and serves in a top corporate position with an internationally recognized company. My roots are in poverty-stricken Appalachia. I have successfully built and now operate several radio stations. We never voted for Clinton/Gore . . . Just thought you might like a snapshot of some of your fans.

Charles Thompson
Bowling Green, KY
(p.164)

#36
Dear Mr. Drudge,
I was exposed to your online news site last year by my father. I was extremely impressed with the reports you put out . . . information that was never before available to the general public. I suppose this is because the execs at the major news outlets were too scared or for that matter didn't want to hurt the agendas they were privately serving. I am proud to see a new generation of Americans like myself growing up without their knowledge of the news being clouded by the Walter Cronkites of yesteryear. Please continue to serve the informed public that you have helped to bring about.

Sincerely,
Geoff Chudleigh
Student at Texas A&M University Class of '00
(p. 168)

#37

Dear Matt,

Since February 1997, when I found your reports on the Web at http://www.drudgereport.com, I have depended on your culling of emerging events from around the world. I rooted for you in front of the Washington Press Club in June 1998, when you responded to every curveball with wit and verve. <u>I listen to your radio show on RealAudio every Sunday night</u>. You are the preeminent knowledge broker of our day, empowering the individual over the corporations—that basic principle of democracy, and making current the old adage that the best things in life are free.

Ken Morrill

(p. 168)

#38

The Drudge Report is the place I sign on to first, when I go online. I can always count on being entertained and informed. <u>I will see stories not offered through the major media outlets, because they think I need to be spoon-fed only with information that fits their political or social agenda.</u> The Drudge Report keeps me street-wise to what is really going on, and the links provided allow me to investigate stories further on my own. Way to go, Matt!

Clifford Jones

16211 North Ravenswood

Magnolia, TX

(p. 175)

#39

Matt,

Thank you for showing that one person can make a difference. For not backing down no matter what pressure is applied by corrupt officials or corporate media elite. For bringing truth to light no matter what the consequences to the powerful, who feel they are above the law or even morality. You are an inspiration for all who felt themselves too small and insignificant to stand up to oppressors. <u>You show that the internet can empower those who dare to do great things.</u>

Mark Reiff

Houston, TX

(p. 178)

#40

<u>DAVOS used the wrong tense.</u> Drudge Report HAS ALREADY changed the world. One citizen's little no-frills website kept "the most powerful man in the world" accountable. It started a media chain reaction that changed the course of cable broadcasting, the government, history writers, and voters to take notice of THE EMPEROR'S STAINED CLOTHES for an entire year. For at least 1 out of 8 years, this wicked ruler was humiliated and proved a craven liar, time after time, with many proofs that history will record.

What do you do for an encore? Who needs an encore!! Just keep up the great work.

Jim
New Lenox, IL
(p. 178)

#41

Dear Matt,

I am a stay at home mom to four kids. I have been reading your report for two years now. In fact, it is one of the few things that I check on every day. Sometimes, several times a day. Your report and its links have kept me in touch with the outside world. Even though there have been times when the information on your site has been removed because of being incorrect, I loved it. I have been able to see what rumors and lies have been going on in and around this country. You have provided an outlet to me that has changed my world. <u>No longer do soaps "entertain" me,</u> I am able to learn and laugh and cry from the information you supply on the real world. Keep up the good work and please continue on until the next millennium!

Kathy Potts
(p. 178)

#42

Dear Mr. Drudge,

After several years of monitoring your website on a daily basis, I recently watched the internet-video of your speech at the National Press Club. I found it to be a striking, well delivered, and thought provoking address. You should be encourageded for the way you challenge the traditional media and journalism.

The list of stories that major news outlets reported inaccurately, was very eye-opening.

I also appreciate your sense that a new era is dawning, which is empowering the individual. I hope it is not a cliché by now to repeat—The internet is boldly changing the world. No one knows where this major shift will take us or how long it will take to get there. But I'm encouraged and have only minor concerns. Congratulations for being on the cutting edge of an exciting revolution where common citizens are gaining the trust of the American people, over major media outlets.

I was stunned on April 20, 1999, as I casually checked your website, the way I do 3–6 times a day. What in the world?! There is a shooting going on right now at Columbine High School, a 15 minute drive from my office where I read your website. What does this say about the power of the internet and the citizen journalist. I'm in south Denver just miles from the site and I hear about a major news story occuring right now from a citizen's website.

This reminded me of a story I heard shortly after President Reagan was shot. It took about a week for London to hear of President Lincoln's assasination in 1865. In 1981, a reporter in London called and informed a friend, a block away from the White House that Reagan had just been shot.

Now in 1998, you had a four day exclusive that Newsweek wouldn't run a story about President Clinton and some young intern named Monica. Then in 1999, I hear about Columbine as it is occuring, in my own city, on the Drudge Report.

Since then, I've told my friends and family—"If you want to know what is going on right now, the latest and the greatest, you need to check one place—the Drudge Report." Many have thanked me since. It makes me wonder when you sleep, Matt!

These days more than ever, I believe in multiple news and sources to better my chances of learning "the facts." It is my belief that this assists us in grasping that sometimes elusive commodity—the truth. The Drudge Report is at the top of my list and you've also got my radio recorder running every Sunday night. More great work. Congratulations on your success and groundbreaking status. It must feel good to put your number of hits up against the other major players on the net. I guess that's one reason why the World Economic Forum just named your

website one of "Ten Websites That will Change the World."
Again congratulations and keep it up. I'll be surfing.
    Chad Osmon
    Denver, CO
    (p. 181)

#43
    Matt Drudge's daily report on world events (and/or just what
he finds interesting) holds considerably more significance than is
often acknowledged. If a major newspaper had the integrity and
variety of reporting and resources that make The Drudge Report a
pleasure to visit every day, it would still only be a great paper. The
true significance of the Drudge report is rooted in the significance
of the uniqueness of the American vision. Such a lofty statement
in reference to a web site? No, not if one considers not only the
impact Matt alone has had on the world, but maybe more so, on
what he represents. Just as the Christian vision, according to St.
Paul, was to "Be of one mind," so was it the American ideal to be
one people, under God. That is, all equal in having fair play
simply because we are alive, and not by any dictates of any one
or group who hold over the power of death. You see, by Matt
reporting on what he alone cares about, and only what he cares
about, he is in a sense speaking for all people. This is what
makes The Drudge Report uniquely significant. He cares in
relation to the dictates of only himself, and not being motivated
through fear by anyone or group/organization over him. For as
George Macdonald wrote, "All wickedness tends to destroy
individuality and declining natures assimilate as they sink." This is
not to say that it is impossible for big corporate news giants to
report important goings on in our lives. It's just that by nature,
they can not do it very well. There is a purity in individuality
that they can never hope to achieve, any more than a camel
through the eye of a needle.
    Jean-Pierre Henderson
    Chicago, IL
    (p. 182)

#44
    DrudgeReport is just one of the first websites which is
revolutionizing the way people of this world will receive their
news. I know it's changed my habits for news, such that I no

longer rely on the staid and leftist drivel from the TV. I believe that Matt Drudge's website is showing the way for the web and those that understand and act on it will be the Matt Drudges or the Time Warners in the future. First sites will cater to specific interests. This site could have news and links solely for those seeking news about Farmers and Agriculture. Another site might just give you news related to the New World Order. The old media must adjust to the changes or they will be buried by them within a couple years. It's obvious to anyone who has been to the DrudgeReport, WorldNetDaily or Free Republic that the news business has a lot of changing to do if they are to even survive. People will seek to find "gate-keepers" that they trust, knowing that those gates are never locked. You will never be forced to make do with what's on the TV news or in the paper, which is very limited compared with the wealth of information available online. So how long will the Washington Posts and New York Timeses of the world last after the internet has entered every home? They probably don't in their present forms. Those newspapers will have to shrink their size and scope while admitting their biases and aiming for that audience which agrees with them. Before newspapers vanish we will see many small newspapers appear across the country and planet. Many of those will resemble websites with banner ads. Television? What's that? Today there are free internet services in abundance in this and other countries which rely on ads. Those services are usually at speeds of 28K but soon those that aren't DSL will find their markets shrinking. After that it's only a matter of time before we are all watching our favorite dramas and sci-fi programs via the net. Probably connected to a TV in a way as to allow you to use it as easily as cable. Imagine 3,000 channels all available to everyone at nothing, provided you have a phone line. <u>Matt Drudge is far from dead!</u> Matt Drudge is on the leading edge of the revolution which shall sweep America and the world into a new information age. The old media is almost dead and doesn't seem to have much of a clue as to what to do about it yet. In the soon to be issued final edition of the New York Times I expect to see an editorial or a front page story saying "Should have listened to Drudge."

Floyd Looney
Texas
(p. 182)

#45

Matt,

I believe the Drudge Report stands as revolutionary for our world today as Gutenberg's printing press did for his world. <u>No longer did the common people have to take the word of the Church as to what they should believe.</u> They had access to find out on their own what was contained in the pages of the Bible. It gave them freedom to believe what they found was the truth. Today, the Drudge Report allows the common people to have access in a similar fashion. No longer do we have to rely on our sole source of news and information coming out of the politically motivated Establishment. It is freedom to be able to cut through the confusing lies and propaganda to find the truth. It is a triumph for the advancement of truth if information can make its way out to millions of people even if the traditional media chooses to become a censor. It is a freedom that can be enjoyed by anyone in the world no matter how oppressed as long as they have access to the internet. That is why the Drudge Report is truly revolutionary.

Bryan Hiler

Osceola, IN

(P.S. Keep up the great work, don't get burned out. In his time Gutenberg was persecuted, now he is hailed as one of the greatest people of a millennium.)

(p. 190)

#46

About the supposed ugliness of the Drudge Report website . . .

Being an art director and graphic designer—and a French one at that!—for the last 10 years, I felt the urge to give my opinion on the Drudge Report's aesthetic.

This simple stand-alone page of links couldn't be better designed than as it is: a simple listing. I do not see a sincere alternative. The simplicity of its look is its best feature; it has become part of the vernacular. <u>As with all efficient design, the Drudge Report seems timeless, and has become a parameter of our visual electronic landscape.</u>

Your use of the variable font makes each reader his or her own designer. I guess you have been contacted by 1,000 or more designers proposing to update the site . . . Don't! Too many ugly, trendy, over-the-top and meaningless sites are proliferating and polluting the web.

As long as the Drudge Report's design continues to represent its substance—wherein design doesn't become more dominant than content—it will remain a graphic icon of our times.

Marc Atlan
Venice, CA, USA
(p. 191)

EPILOGUE

WHO'S WATCHING DARIUS?

WASHINGTON—"Do you have any champagne?" CNN60-MINUTES all-star Christiane Amanpour asked the bartender at the BLOOMBERG after-party as she giggled with her husband Jamie Rubin who wore no black-tie even though the invitation required it.

"All the rebels have become conformists," I later said to Amanpour as we sat and talked about the sell-out.

With Jamie rolling his eyes, I accused Amanpour of blindly supporting The State, as I donned a T-shirt of an ironed-on Elian Gonzalez at gunpoint [copyright Alan Diaz, ASSOCIATED PRESS].

"That's just horrible you're wearing thaaaat," Amanpour said in between sips in an accent that spans the continents.

"All you rebels have become conformists," I repeated. "HE did this to you!"

For a moment in the BLOOMBERG bathroom I had a panic attack. It hit me hard. HE will soon be gone.

Not just Jamie, not just Lockhart, not just Janet, not just Madeleine, not just Sidney, and not just Amanpour, who apparently timed her pollination to his leaving.

HE is their center.

And, Christiane, who's watching baby Darius?

HE seduced them. HE loved them. HE gave them good copy. HE was their friend. USA TODAY all-star Susan Page presented him with an Oscar. A few weeks ago in Beverly Hills Jay Leno presented him with a check.

"They'll never indict him," Sam Donaldson screamed, with a voice nearly recovered from yelling at Reagan.

TIME editor Isaacson was laughing so hard, sitting next to Madeleine, please forgive if the magazine is tear-stained Monday.

Because HE is leaving. And HE corrupted them.

Lord of the Baby Boom.

What will we all do without him?

"We're going to miss you, Mr. President," I said, leaning over the velvet rope flashing my Elian T with him, looking up and down, glaring at me.

"How did he get in here," press maestro Joe Lockhart whispered into the ear of a reporter while chewing a mouth full of spicy greens, mango and lo mein noodles served with warm sesame crusted salmon, grilled lamb chop and sliced tenderloin of beef, sauce cabernet, potato dauphinoise rondelle, baby carrots and asparagus, french rolls, flat breads, pumpernickel, raisin rolls, marble mousse torte, chocolate crust filled with white chocolate and semi-sweet chocolate mousse, fresh fruit garnish and coffee.

Janet stared in horror as I stood in front of her—Elian, with his look of horror, staring her straight back in her face.

"You're my homepage. I read you all the time. I love it when you put up a siren. You made me a star, honey. I have to get a picture with you," said Smear Queen Diva and campaign manager to Al Gore Donna Brazile as we hugged and talked about what a fun 2000 we're going to have.

But HE will never be replaced.

Dean of the Degenerates.

Leno showed a video of a dog dry humping a woman's leg—then quickly flashed a pic of the Commander in Chief.

The crowd cheers. So does his wife. And so does HE.

As does Lockhart, while chewing a mouthful of Rivercrest Chardonnay, Rivercrest Cabernet Sauvignon.

Impeached. Stained. Accused. Standing Ovation.

The highlight of the night, this his final formal night with family at the WHITE HOUSE CORRESPONDENTS DINNER, was a video of "Ken Starr" smoking a cigar, dressed in drag, flashing his underwear, harboring an apparent erection.

As the crowd roared and Wolf howled and Janet clapped her wings.

Deputy Attorney General Eric Holder would later tell me after the lights came on and the crowd began dispersing and the HILTON staff began sweeping up all the wet Kleenex: "It was in good humor."

"You have the impeached president and the gentleman assigned, by Justice, who proved the case now depicted in drag, in his underwear, obviously aroused, as presidential staffers who spread Starr gay rumors celebrate?! And that's good taste? Good humor?" I press Holder, flashing my Elian.

"Do you have any champagne?" Amanpour asked the bartender at BLOOMBERG.

"Darling, here it's flowing in the streets."

Goodbye, Bill Clinton.

XXX